636.1083

X W

KT-551-952

MODERN
STABLE
MANAGEMENT

Ward Lock Riding School

KNOW YOUR PONY
UNDERSTANDING YOUR HORSE
LEARNING TO RIDE
DISCOVERING DRESSAGE
EVENTING
PRACTICAL SHOWJUMPING
TACK AND CLOTHING
UNDERSTANDING FITNESS AND TRAINING

MODERN STABLE MANAGEMENT

SUSAN McBANE

WARD LOCK
RIDING SCHOOL

WARD LOCK

This book is dedicated to
RA
a dog and a half

A WARD LOCK BOOK

First published in the UK 1994
by Ward Lock
A Cassell Imprint
Wellington House
125 Strand
London
WC2R 0BB

Copyright © Susan McBane 1994
First paperback edition 1998

Distributed in the United States
by Sterling Publishing Co., Inc.
387 Park Avenue South, New York, NY 10016-8810

A British Library Cataloguing in Publication Data block for
this book may be obtained from the British Library

ISBN 0-7063-7699-4

Typeset by Litho Link Ltd, Welshpool, Powys, Wales

Printed and bound in Great Britain by Hillman Printers (Frome) Ltd

Frontispiece: *A well-managed horse should appear interested in its surroundings. Most horses prefer being stabled where they can see what is going on.*

CONTENTS

	Introduction	6
1	Management Methods	7
2	The Horse's Basic Needs	13
3	Feeding	21
4	Feet and Shoes	34
5	Bedding	41
6	Skin and Coat	46
7	Tack and Clothing	57
8	Accommodating Horses	66
9	Exercise and Work	72
10	Psychology and Handling	75
11	Health Topics	81
12	Travelling	88
	Index	95

INTRODUCTION

This book has not been written for complete beginners, but for horse owners who already have a basic, conventional knowledge of horse management and who wish to learn more about the principles of horse and pony care and management. Some of the advice contained here may not be what you have previously been taught but all of it is soundly based on scientific fact. Veterinary research in equine topics continues, thanks largely to funding from the racing world and commercial companies, with input from other sources. Some of it shows that certain practices, long held to be valid, are, in fact, not so and that some traditional practices may even be actually bad for the horse.

I hope that readers will find this book enlightening and that it will encourage them not to accept blindly everything they may have been taught but to think about what they do with and to their horses and ponies and to seek alternative expert advice when in doubt.

CHAPTER 1

MANAGEMENT METHODS

One well-worn, yet true, saying in the horse world, that is often overlooked or ignored, is that each horse is an individual and must be treated as such. The basic tenets of good horse management obviously provide a framework of suitable policies to guide most horse owners and managers but the real trick to successful horse care and management is to recognize your horse's individualities, both physical and mental, and then to adapt your stable routine not only to suit the horse but also to take into account your own lifestyle and family needs.

For example, it is no use choosing a horse that needs a lot of work and care if you are extremely busy and have strictly limited time for horse matters. Likewise, there is no point in deciding to adopt a fairly trouble-free method of caring for your horse, such as keeping it out at grass most, or all, of the time, if it is the sort of animal that will not thrive in this type of life. You will save yourself much anxiety if you give careful thought to these matters and establish what facilities and how much time you are able to offer before you buy your horse or pony.

WHICH METHOD TO CHOOSE?

There are four main ways of keeping horses:

U Stabled all or most of the time;

U Out at grass all, or most, of the time;

U On a combined system (a combination of those two methods);

U Yarding or 'open stabling' (where the animals are kept together in compatible groups in large, surfaced or bedded-down enclosures, either indoors or with access to an outdoor area as well, or even with access to pasture.

STABLED HORSES AND PONIES

These animals are complete prisoners. Not only do they have no freedom but they are completely dependent on their human attendants for absolutely everything – exercise, food, water, clothing, grooming, environmental control and access to company, the latter often being denied them.

These days, stabled horses are mostly kept in loose boxes (box stalls in the USA), although stalls (standing stalls in the USA) can still be found, particularly in police and military yards and in some commercial premises, such as breweries.

With stabled animals, it is best to establish a fairly strict stable routine to ensure that everything is done, nothing is overlooked, and that the horses, who have very little to occupy them, know what to expect and when. This places a considerable burden of responsibility and time on whoever is caring for the horse and is obviously very tying. This person must also make time available to exercise the horse, this being one commodity of which stabled animals invariably go very short. It is generally accepted that about two

hours' exercise daily is sufficient for a healthy horse, to keep both body and mind ticking over in good shape, but, in fact, this is probably far too little.

Natural social contact is another commodity that stabled animals often lack. Being kept in individual boxes, they may not even have 'chat holes' or grilles in their boxes so that they can 'talk' to their neighbours. Indeed, many reputable texts expressly forbid this, along with permitting horses to communicate over their box doors.

Knowing that there are animals in neighbouring stables and being able to see them (if not touch them) does, obviously, help a great deal and most horses come to accept this lifestyle with a reasonable amount of contentment, regarding their stables as 'home' where they know they will find safety, food, water and bedding. It is when the confinement is

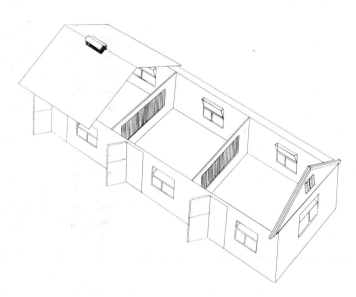

A row of conventional loose boxes with various horse-friendly features to improve them. The ridge roof ventilators help to ensure adequate air change. Inside, the horses can see and socialize with each other through the grilles and there are windows and ventilation devices on all the outside walls.

excessive (or the exercise too little, which amounts to the same thing), when contact with other horses is minimal, when there is little to interest the horse and when it is hungry for much of the time (a condition suffered by many stabled horses and one that is completely unnatural for them and which can be dangerous) that the system fails. When this happens it is the fault of the people running the system, not of the system itself, as they have not administered it according to the horse's real needs.

From the horse's point of view, being stabled in inclement weather is certainly better than being left to tough it out in an exposed field (even hardy native ponies like and need shelter), while from the owner's point of view, the stabled horse is always handy, easier to keep clean and able to be fed exactly as the owner sees fit. However, it is not true that only stabled horses can be made fit for hard work.

KEEPING A HORSE OR PONY AT GRASS

This is much less labour-intensive than stabling it entirely. There is no mucking out, no precisely strict feeding times, no compulsion to exercise the horse unless you are training or conditioning it and no thorough body brushing when grooming, although you should still check the horse twice a day (many owners don't), dandy it over, sponge face and dock, pick out feet and feed it when appropriate. The horse will always be dirtier than a stabled horse and if your grazing is at all rich it may

easily become too fat and soft for fitness to be achieved.

On the credit side, provided it has congenial company and truly effective shelter, it will certainly be healthier (as opposed to fitter) and more content than a stabled horse. This, in itself, is a weight off a conscientious owner's mind and a boost to the horse's wellbeing and outlook on life – benefits not to be dismissed lightly.

THE COMBINED SYSTEM

This is the one that offers the best of both worlds. The horse spends part of the day stabled and part at grass. In practice, the best system is for the horse to be out during the daylight hours in winter (probably when its owner is at school or work), coming in at night to a thick, clean, dry bed and a good feed, and being out at night in summer, away from the heat and flies, and stabled in the shade and cool during the day. However, much depends on your routine and requirements. You can obviously vary the in-and-out hours as much as you wish.

The advantages are that the horse has the shelter, privacy, peace and quiet of its stable when needed but also gets plenty of opportunity to exercise and play in the paddock and is able to enjoy the natural social company of other horses (provided it is not turned out alone). Most horses really thrive on this system of management. They can be made very fit (again, if the grass is not over-rich), kept clean and fed a reasonably controlled diet. They are normally happy and healthy on this system.

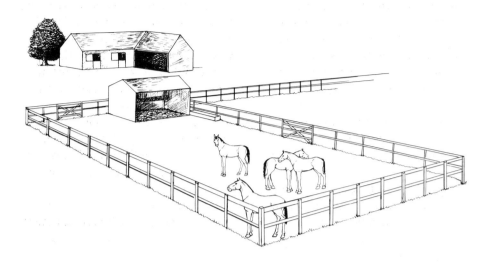

A surfaced exercise area with a shelter containing bedding and hay, and water nearby. The horses have access to the grass paddock through the gate and, when ground conditions are bad, they can be confined to the fenced-in area.

YARDING

This is coming more into favour and is an excellent system. The animals are kept in large, covered barns or partly roofed enclosures, the surfaces of which are either normal bedding or something such as earth, fine shale, woodchips, etc. They can be kept in entirely (depending on the design of the yard), be allowed to wander in and out of the outdoor area or even given access to pasture as well, which is the best system from the horse's point of view. They must be kept in mixed groups of friendly horses and it does not matter if they are shod as horses that are used to each other and living in this way will rarely kick or injure each other, even in play. (This also goes for animals turned out regularly together for a few hours from loose boxes.)

Horses kept in this way can be made extremely fit, kept clean, as the materials used for surfacing enclosures brush off easily, and can have their diets minutely controlled. They benefit from the natural, social company, the space and freedom needed by all horses, exercise taken at will and the moral support of constant company from their peers.

THE LEGACY OF EVOLUTION

A cursory glance at even the smallest competitors at any horse show will confirm that horses and ponies come in all sorts, shapes and sizes. They all have one thing in common, however – they evolved as grazing, running animals whose natural home was, and is, wide open plains. Much further back in time, the horse's ancestors were forest animals and, like other forest animals, horses are often good, natural jumpers. Probably the one factor welding them all together is that the horse family has always been preyed upon by others. Even horses from families that have been domesticated for thousands of years still have a prey animal's physique and mentality. They have been domesticated for only about 5,000 years and you cannot undo over 50 million years of evolution in so short a time.

This all means that the horse as an individual needs space and freedom to run away from any perceived danger, has a basically nervous nature (even apparently 'bombproof' ponies and police horses can go berserk when the circumstances are right), needs feeding as if it had a constant supply of grass if its digestive system and brain are to function well and requires the security of a herd environment, even if it cannot be with its peers all the time, if it is to be calm and content and able to thrive physically.

There is also one other factor to consider and that is the environment

Evolution

Animals whose ancestors evolved in hot, dry parts of the world have particular physical characteristics that help them to survive in such an environment. They have long legs in relation to their height to allow good air movement around the body, thin skin, with blood vessels near the surface, to facilitate the loss of excess heat by radiation, extra sweat glands in the skin to facilitate heat loss through evaporation and widely flaring nostrils to get rid of heat by exhaling warm, 'used air' and water vapour. They have short heads because long air passages intended to warm up the air entering the body via the nostrils are not necessary; their ears are longish in relation to head size, again to facilitate heat loss as the ears have a rich blood supply, and their tail carriage is usually high and held away from the body, which facilitates the circulation of air around the body and thus the removal of excess body heat. Their coats are shorter and thinner at all times of year, not only to prevent

the retention of heat but also because they do not need the same protection against the cold and wet as their relatives from colder climes.

Horses and ponies that have evolved in colder regions have the opposite physical characteristics. Their ears are short, to conserve body heat, and their heads are large and long so that inhaled air can be warmed up before reaching the lungs. Their legs are shorter and their barrels more rounded, another heat-retaining characteristic. Their tail carriage is usually low, with the tail set on lower so that the dock is held down between the buttocks most of the time, protecting this thin-skinned area which loses heat easily. Their coats are thicker and longer to insulate the body against cold and, to some extent, wet, and their mane and tail hair is coarser and sometimes wavy or even curly, which increases the amount of warm air trapped between the hairs close to the body. They have narrower, slit-like nostrils, their skin is thicker and they have fewer sweat glands.

An Arab horse, a good example of the type of horse that evolved in hot areas of the world. Other breeds are the Turkmene, the Caspian, and the Thoroughbred which is descended from Oriental types, mainly Arabs and Barbs.

A Przewalski horse showing 'cold area' characteristics. The Przewalski is related to the domestic horse Equus caballus, but it is not thought to be a direct relationship because they have a different number of chromosomes.

in which the domesticated, family horse or pony's most immediate wild ancestors evolved. Our planet has various elements of climate and the horse can, and does, live in most of them. The further away from a horse's natural climate and environment you take it, the more problems you will have in looking after it and the less likely it is to thrive.

Animals whose ancestors evolved in hot, dry areas should not be forced to live out during a northern hemisphere winter. Although the British climate is classed as temperate, winters can be miserable, cold and wet, and this is not suitable weather in which to winter out animals of Thoroughbred, Arab or Caspian blood without very good shelter, thick rugs and extra feeding to keep out the cold and wet. Wet and wind multiply the effects of the cold, making such a climate much

worse for animals to bear than very cold but drier conditions.

If your situation is such that you have little time for horse care and you cannot, or do not wish to, keep your horse at livery, you would be well advised to buy an animal with many natural, native characteristics suited to your area of the world, so that you can keep it mainly out and it will not be unduly affected by the climate. If your heart is set on an animal with Thoroughbred, Arab or Caspian blood, however, even a part-bred, you will have to make sure that you can provide adequate facilities for effective shelter, exercise, clothing and feeding, as well as the other basic elements of care, if it is to thrive and not deteriorate in condition and maybe start costing you a good deal in veterinary bills. It is obviously cruel to force an animal to endure conditions for which it is not suited.

CHAPTER 2

THE HORSE'S BASIC NEEDS

To keep a horse healthy and contented an owner or manager must consider six basic things: food, water, shelter, company, personal space and freedom to move around. Of course, readers will be able to think of various other essentials, such as farriery and veterinary services, clothing and useful equipment, but, here, I am looking at the basic needs of horses, things they have enjoyed for millions of years and which shaped the horse into the animals we know today. Catering properly for these six needs will go a long way towards maintaining a healthy, happy horse but, in practice, I find that some people's interpretation of just how to provide them for domesticated horses often falls far short of the horse's actual requirements.

FOOD

In common with most other grazing and browsing animals, the horse is a trickle feeder, which has evolved to survive best with an almost constant supply of food passing through its digestive system in small amounts. The horse is not a ruminant like a cow, which takes in fairly large quantities of food and swallows it almost at once, regurgitating it later as cud to chew at its leisure. The horse chews the grass as it goes along and then swallows it, never to be seen again until the undigested remains emerge as droppings.

Grass, leaves and other herbage are high in fibre (roughage) and water but contain relatively few nutrients in proportion to the bulk consumed. This means that the horse is designed to take in large quantities of fibre and water and its digestive system has evolved to cope well with this situation. The stomach itself is fairly small but the system as a whole is very capacious. In fact, it has reached the point where it cannot function satisfactorily *without* large quantities of bulky roughage.

As we feed them, concentrates are alien to the horse's digestive system. True, in natural conditions feral horses will come across cereals, either growing or lying as grain on the ground, but these natural species of grain-producing plants are much less 'rich' than our purpose-bred genetically manipulated species. A highly concentrated, rich diet of this type is not natural to the horse and can be the cause of many physical or behavioural problems in domesticated horses, such as swollen, inflamed joints in youngstock, colic, 'corn sickness', where horses that have been over-fed on concentrates go off their feed because of chronic slight indigestion, crazy behaviour due to an excessive intake of energy-rich foods which cause high levels of toxins to circulate in the body, affecting both metabolism and behaviour, azoturia, lymphangitis and other disorders.

To use up the high levels of energy often created in stabled, working horses, particularly in cobs and ponies, *far* more exercise or work is needed than is often given to most privately owned animals and many commercially used ones, too.

If you feed a conventional diet of hay and 'shorts' or 'straights' (concentrates such as oats, barley, cubes or coarse mix), in order to feed the horse as naturally as such a method will allow, yet still give it the nutrients necessary for hard work, your best plan is to use the best quality hay you can possibly get and build up the concentrates on top of that, rather than regarding hay as an 'extra' to back up high levels of concentrates. It would be well worth the once-only fee charged by a competent equine nutritionist to have your hay, and the rest of what you propose feeding, analysed, so that you can compile the best diet for your horse.

Hayage (moist, vacuum-packed forage) is often used instead of hay these days and has the advantage of having such an analysis printed on the bag. However, at the time of writing the biggest breakthrough is the emergence of 'forage' feeds, which enable the horse to be trickle-fed as nature intended. These feeds

are 'dry' (like hay and chop) or slightly moist and dust-free and are formulated so that even quite hard-working horses will get everything they need from them without requiring extra concentrates. The firms producing these feeds also frequently produce 'booster' feeds of various sorts, which can be added to the diets of hard-working, athletic horses or breeding stock.

Your aim should be to give the horse a more or less constant supply of good hay, hayage or a forage feed, with extra concentrates given as frequently as possible each day, if needed. Feeding hay *ad lib* is nothing new. Wise horsemasters have done it for generations but it does not seem to be a popular system now in our teaching establishments and other organizations, the result being that thousands of horses and ponies are kept for many hours each day with *no food* at all available to them – a highly unnatural and dangerous situation for an animal with a digestive system like that of a horse. It is no wonder that colic and other digestive and behavioural problems that stem from indigestion, physical discomfort, mental frustration and boredom are so common.

Of course, the horse should not be fed just before work, but the outdated practice of removing all feed and water for several hours before physical exertion is quite wrong, damaging to the horse and cruel.

WATER

Depending on its age and condition, the horse's body may be composed of up to 70 per cent water. Water is contained in most parts of the body. A body without water is just so much dust.

In the wild, equidae often trek many miles to find water and certain populations of zebra have developed the ability to go for several days between drinks in hot climates. Observations of feral horses and ponies indicate that they seem to prefer drinking in the morning and evening and will journey to water sources at those times if their feeding area is not near water.

Domesticated horses usually have access to water all the time and this is fine. Most owners will notice that their horse does not only drink in the morning and evening but whenever it feels like it, and feral animals grazing near water will do this too. Water is now believed to stimulate the digestive juices, not to hamper digestion as was once thought. Students are still usually taught not to give horses water immediately after a full feed but, in practice, it is found that horses that always have water by them often take a short drink immediately after a feed and sometimes during a feed, while some dunk their hay in their water, with absolutely no ill effects whatsoever. In fact, some vets and nutritionists feel that depriving a horse of water at feeding times may encourage indigestion if not actual colic.

It is also now known to be bad for horses to be denied water for hours before hard work such as a competitive event. They can safely drink up to an hour before hard work (it passes quickly through their digestive system) and this will help prevent dangerous dehydration. This is especially important in warm or hot weather.

If, for some reason, you cannot provide fresh water for your horses all the time, it will be quite safe to let them drink their fill at least twice a day. As they will probably take a couple of long draughts at these times (in hot weather a horse may need up to 55 litres (12 gallons) of water a day, depending on its work), it would be safest to let them drink before feeding in the case of stabled animals. Grass-kept horses do not gorge themselves on their ever-present food, so they can be watered without worrying about this.

When horses are led to water in this way, they will often take a long drink, then raise their heads and have a rest, perhaps looking about them. Do not take this as a cue that they have finished. Wait, and you will almost certainly find that they take another long drink before moving away from the water of their own accord. Only then can you be sure they have fully quenched their thirst.

For grass-kept or yarded horses, water can be supplied in troughs that are plumbed in or filled by hosepipe. A popular, cheap and safe method of watering horses in fields without piped water is to tie a clean plastic dustbin to the fence and fill it by hosepipe – but do keep it topped up as, if the water level drops too low, the horses may not try to reach it.

Stabled horses can have automatic waterers or buckets in holders to prevent them from being knocked over.

Whatever container you use, it must be kept clean. Stable buckets and auto-waterers should be scrubbed out with clean water daily and a field trough cleared out monthly. Whatever method you use, the water must be clean, fresh and readily available.

SHELTER

Surprisingly, this is one aspect of management that is often overlooked. Whenever you mention field shelters, you will invariably hear a chorus of: 'Oh, my horse never uses one.' My experience, in over 45 years with horses, is that, almost without exception, they will *all* use a shelter:
(a) when they feel the need;
(b) providing that they are not afraid to do so – and this latter point is most important!

In fields and paddocks a shelter shed should have its back to the prevailing wind on the highest (and therefore driest) part of the field, preferably with an open aspect as horses do not like being closed in. The entrance should be high, wide and welcoming, and the shed should be light inside (perhaps by means of a leakproof, polythene panel). It is nice to keep it bedded down, skipped out daily, and, according to grass availability, permanently stocked with good hay in racks or nets so that the horses come to regard it as a haven from the weather and flies, where they can lie down and rest in comfort and where they will usually find fresh food waiting, according to the season.

The entrance should be well above horse's head height and it is usual to have the whole of the front, on the side away from the prevailing wind, open, so that the horses are not afraid

of knocking themselves as they go in or being trapped once inside.

Most types of wild horse or pony live in an environment where there is some form of shelter, and equidae the world over have become adept at seeking out dips in the ground, learning the windflow routes, finding shrubbery, cliffs, trees, hedges or whatever else they can get under or behind to escape the worst of the wind, snow, driving or pouring rain, sun or insects. It is unnatural for them to be totally exposed to the elements and bad management to force a domesticated horse to endure such conditions. At most times of the year, a domesticated horse or pony that is turned out for more than just a few hours a day (and maybe even then, depending on the conditions) must have access to effective side-on and overhead shelter if it is to be comfortable.

A sturdy, roomy shelter shed for two horses should be about 5.5 m (18 ft) wide and at least half that measurement deep. A horse can attain a height of roughly 3.4 m (10½ ft) if it rears and although it may not be prone to doing this indoors, it is something to think about. Lack of room or height in a shed is a common reason for horses not daring to use it.

'Natural' shelter in domesticated conditions will probably be restricted to hedges and trees. Again, you have to consider the direction of the prevailing wind across your fields. If the wind blows from the west, it is no good expecting a hedge on the east side of the field to act as a weatherbreak! In summer, broad-leaved trees offer welcome shade (but

This paddock offers no shelter at all to its unfortunate inhabitants. The post and rail fencing is useless for this purpose and the only hedge cannot be used as protection from the wind. There is no shelter shed.

no respite from flies) but in winter both hedges and trees are fairly useless if they lose their leaves. Whatever natural shelter you have, unless it is truly exceptional, I still feel that a good shelter shed and the use of an effective fly repellent in summer (one that states on the pack that its effects last for days) are the best ways to protect domesticated horses from the elements.

Horses suffering from exposure lose condition very quickly. They can suffer fom hypothermia in winter and from heatstroke in summer. In bad weather they fall prey to mud fever and rain scald and get chapped, sore faces caused by runny eyes. In hot weather, they are positively tortured by flies, which may cause eye infections, and get jarred legs or broken hooves from the hard ground.

Good shelter is an essential part of good horse and pony management and is cheaper in the long run than putting right an afflicted horse.

SPACE

Like many other creatures, horses maintain a strongly felt personal space around them, which even other horses, let alone alien species like people, intrude upon at their peril. Observing a group of grazing horses will demonstrate to you that the only animals allowed to get really close will be a horse's particular friends, a mare's foal or a stallion who may (or may not) be allowed close to a mare in season.

Because of the shape of the horse's body, the invisible border of its personal space seems to be oval in

Company

There are *very* few horses who truly do not mind being alone, far fewer than are actually kept alone by owners who maintain that they don't mind and seem fine. My experience of formerly lone horses and ponies is that, almost with exception, they become physically healthier, easier to keep and noticeably more content when given company of their own kind. Some people do give them donkeys, goats or young cattle for company but this is not really the same as another horse or pony.

Horses are herd animals and their whole evolution is geared to this sort of life. There is safety in numbers and they still instinctively feel this. Our animals may not be preyed on by wild cats and hyenas but they still retain the instinct to herd together for safety.

Of course, horses have to learn to work alone but this is quite different from being kept in solitary confinement or being turned out alone.

Although some horses do get used to this unhappy state of affairs, many do not and may constantly get into trouble through trying to jump out to go in search of other horses, or wandering up and down fences and pining by gates.

Conscientious owners and managers always take into account the horse's mental as well as its physical needs and company is one of the greatest. Even when horses are kept mainly stabled, being turned out daily with congenial company should be an important part of their routine, not regarded as a special treat when it is convenient.

Horses nearly always thrive in company. Even if turned out alone, a neighbouring horse is better than no company at all, provided the horses are compatible. Here the fencing is at back height and there is a rail on the far side running at shoulder height to protect the far horse from injury on exposed posts.

shape and extends to around 4.2 m (14 ft) around the horse. It will be obvious at once that most stables come well inside the horse's natural personal space boundary and this is a significant factor to consider when housing horses. Most people would find it highly impractical to provide loose boxes large enough to take this into account but we can take steps to respect the horse's feelings.

For a start, horses should only be stabled next to friends or, at least, not next to enemies. Even if a horse cannot actually see its neighbour, it will know from the sounds and smell that it is there and it has been scientifically proved that an enemy constantly within its personal space, even if separated by a wall, creates stress that will significantly and adversely affect the horse's contentment, behaviour and physical wellbeing.

There is a common view that two friends should not be stabled near each other as they then form an 'impossibly' strong friendship and create problems when separated for work. In a well-run yard, where the horses know what to expect and more or less when to expect it, they soon learn that separations are temporary. All horses and ponies have to learn to work alone and with competent managers and trainers in charge this is no problem. Denying a horse natural friendship outside working hours is totally unnecessary, foolish and unkind.

If you do have problems with horses who refuse to leave friends, their home environment or whatever, and do not feel able to sort this out yourself, get in a professional trainer for a few sessions to show you how to put matters right. Once they know you have the upper hand, most horses will stop 'trying it on' and you should have no further problems.

The need for space around it is so ingrained in the horse's psyche that it is also well worth remembering that most horses begin to feel insecure or even frightened in small spaces, particularly unfamiliar ones such as a different stable, vehicle or even an indoor school. They may not show it obviously (although an observant eye or sensitive hand on a neck may detect uncertainty or a slight tremble), so don't automatically assume they are calm and accepting. As ever, confidence and quietness in us are valuable cues that many horses will follow if they trust humans.

FREEDOM OF MOVEMENT

Having already mentioned the horse's evolution as a plains animal, this last requirement should not come as a surprise. In the wild its whole lifestyle is nomadic unless the herds live in restricted areas, when they will, of necessity, become static and territorial.

The need for freedom does not mean that horses and ponies at liberty spend a lot of time moving around at faster gaits. Normally, they amble around, grazing, swinging their heads from side to side as they crop the grass. They mostly walk (the old advice to spend most of a horse's exercise period at walk holding good here), do not trot much (a message here for those who spend hours drilling in trot when exercising or schooling) and use canter as a natural gait for travelling from one area to another. Of course, all gaits are also used occasionally during normal social communication and when playing, while gallop is used both during play or when escaping from danger.

It is inappropriate to give the horse a lifestyle comprising about 22 hours a day of confinement and forced idleness in a box, broken up by two hours or less of relatively hard work. This is not a natural state of affairs for the horse, which actually requires just the opposite – several hours a day of steady walking around at liberty for most of that time, with fast or intensive, hard, physical work taking up a very short period of time, depending on the horse's training programme and workload.

If pasture is not available all year round, at least some sort of surfaced exercise area, into which the horses can be turned loose, should be provided, ideally with some kind of shelter shed into which they can wander if the elements are unkind. Most yards have an odd corner that is not being put to much use and which could be rearranged to provide an exercise area or even a 'play pen' into which a couple of animals at a time, or even one if still in view of others, can be turned out to wander about gently, stretch their legs, have a buck and a roll and generally get away from the boredom of the box for a few hours a day.

Many professional or large amateur yards have outdoor *manèges* or indoor schools that could be used for free exercise of this sort when not being used for lessons or schooling – possibly overnight. On suitably surfaced areas without grass, haynets can be hung around and water provided and the horses are normally quite happy.

The horse has six basic requirements:

- ∪ Food – to provide energy and warmth;

- ∪ Water – to help the body's systems to work properly;

- ∪ Shelter from harsh or hot weather and insects;

- ∪ Company of other horses;

- ∪ Personal space;

- ∪ Freedom of movement – horses do not like to be confined.

CHAPTER 3

FEEDING

The horse's basic eating habits and the type of diet that suits it have been discussed in Chapter 2. Unfortunately, the type of diet that many domesticated horses receive, comprising say, three feeds a day or less, often with many hours between them, with roughage, usually given in the form of hay, fed only night and morning, does not imitate its natural method of eating, but is widespread and even taught as correct. In practice, this leaves horses for very many hours with no food at all, a situation that is unnatural to them, creates considerable physical discomfort and boredom, and positively favours 'unexplained' colic and stable vices.

THE DIGESTIVE SYSTEM

As shown in the illustration below, the digestive system of the horse is capacious and is divided into various compartments which have individual jobs to do.

In general, digestion is achieved through the action of various chemicals, enzymes and microscopic organisms (referred to by nutritionists and veterinary surgeons as gut microflora and bacteria) which are crucial to the process. Micro-organisms operate in the large intestine, fermenting and breaking down plant cellulose (a form of carbohydrate or starch present in the horse's natural food and in hay,

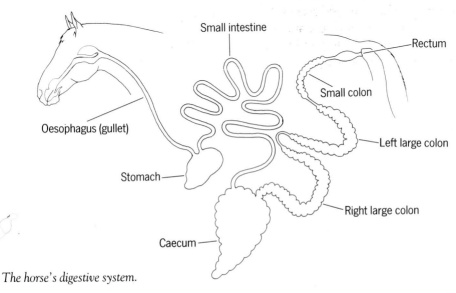

The horse's digestive system.

hayage and some other foods). Because the horse's digestive system is geared to function mainly on this type of food, this fermentation process is obviously vital to the horse's health.

Lignin is another type of bulky material, woody in nature, that is found in grass, hay, feeding straws and so on. It has no nutritional value but is needed to fill out the digestive tract (giving the horse that satisfied feeling we all expect after a meal). Undigested lignin is seen in the droppings as little splinters of fibrous material. If a horse's droppings appear smooth, with little of this material, and barely break on hitting the ground, this may be a sign that the horse is not being fed enough roughage.

If kept on reasonable quality grazing, horses should obtain enough nutrients to do light to moderate work but, as grass is so bulky and needs to be taken in in large amounts for the horse to obtain enough nourishment for hard work, breeding and so on, we have devised more concentrated, artificial methods of feeding, such as hay, oats or barley, or cubes and coarse mixes containing these and various other concentrated foods. This avoids overloading the digestive system and enables us to get the horse's body to work harder than it would in nature. The problem is that the horse finds large amounts of concentrates difficult to digest. In addition, we do not feed the horse tiny, but constant, amounts of concentrates but give relatively large amounts spaced out with several hours between them, which is not a routine the horse's digestive system

can easily cope with.

Because the tiny gut micro-organisms are living creatures, actually living off the horse's own food, they also need a constant supply of food, albeit mainly cellulose. Erratic arrival of food can cause many of them to starve to death or become seriously weakened so that their numbers drop and then they are not available in adequate numbers to process the next lot of food, which may arrive several hours later and the system's efficiency will have been significantly hampered.

To avoid this, horses and ponies should receive an *ad lib* supply of hay or other roughage and, when concentrates are fed, as many small meals per day as possible. Under this system, the organisms responsible for digesting the various foods all have a frequent supply of that food and the horse's system works at its best.

THE CONSTITUENTS OF FOOD

Food is needed to provide fuel for the body to work on. The main food constituents are carbohydrates (starches and sugars), proteins, fats or oils (also called lipids or lipins), vitamins, minerals and trace elements. Water is also essential and has been discussed in Chapter 2.

Carbohydrates
These produce energy and heat, glycogen being the main source of energy. The body stores excess amounts of carbohydrates as fat, in various storage 'depots' around the body, and as glycogen in the muscle cells and the liver.

Proteins

These are the only foods that can make body tissue. The horse's need for protein is lower than was once believed and the protein content is no longer the main criterion when choosing foods, energy levels having taken its place. Excess protein in the diet can be harmful. Although small excesses can be stored as fat, when stored, they lose their tissue-making properties and are then re-used by the body, when called upon, simply as extra energy – an expensive way of providing this.

Fats or oils

Fat produces heat and energy and is 'energy-dense', providing a good feed for very hard-working horses at the limits of their appetites, as it provides one and a half times more energy than carbohydrates.

A fairly high-fat diet may also be prescribed for a very thin horse and fats also help to condition skin, hair and horn, all of which are made of the same basic material.

A high-fat diet is good for horses in endurance-type work such as endurance riding, eventing, hunting and competitive carriage driving or for horses whose owners simply like going for regular, long, active hacks.

Fibre

The importance of fibre has already been explained.

It is the material that makes up the outer husk of grain and the stalks of hay and straw, forming the cell walls and giving plants a shape in the same way our skeleton serves our bodies. Without adequate fibre, roughage or bulk, more concentrated food would clog up into a doughy mass that the digestive juices could not penetrate. It might then begin to ferment or rot inside the horse, the digestive system might impact or block up and the horse could die in agony. Fibre also stimulates peristalsis, the wave-like movements of the digestive tract, which pummel food around and move it along the tract.

Vitamins, minerals and trace elements

Vitamins, minerals and trace elements are vital nutrients that are often needed in only tiny quantities but are essential none the less. All foods contain differing amounts of different ones, with different purposes. Only veterinary surgeons or animal nutritionists are competent to understand their role fully and to devise a diet that is properly balanced for different categories of horse.

Significant mental and physical disorders can arise as a result of deficiencies or overdoses of vitamins, minerals and trace elements, and supplements should never be administered without the advice of a vet, who should take a blood sample and also look at your horse's entire diet, probably having it professionally analysed in a laboratory for absolute accuracy, before deciding which, if any, supplements your animal needs.

If it is decided that you do need a supplement, you must be careful to give it only as advised. Stick to the dose recommended by your vet – feeding less may be pointless and more could be dangerous. Also, never mix different supplements together unless advised to do so by a nutritionist or by your vet.

WHAT IS A BALANCED DIET?

When we speak of a balanced diet, we mean one that contains the correct amounts *and proportions* of the feed constituents mentioned above. As you will have gathered, nutrition is a highly specialized subject and different categories of horse or pony require different kinds of diets. Individuals also vary in their abilities to get the best out of feeds, 'good doers' seeming to need little food to keep them in good condition, compared with 'poor doers' who need more.

How can we hope to choose the correct diet for our horse or pony from among the bewildering variety available? Fortunately, it's not that difficult. The simplest way is to use one of the excellent brand-name products on the market in the form of cubes and/or coarse mixes, together with hayage, or to use one of the newer forage feeds. All reputable companies produce clear information about their products, which should enable you to choose the correct product from their range. They also employ well-qualified nutritionists who should be willing to advise you, free of charge, on how to use the products and which would best suit your animal.

Other sources of help normally charge for their services. These include your veterinary surgeon and (in Britain) the Equine Services Department of your local branch of the Agricultural Development Advisory Service. Also available are qualified individuals who run nutrition consultancies but these

people may be retained by a commercial feed company and so may not be independent and, therefore, unbiased.

It is particularly important to get specialist advice if you do not wish to use a branded feed but prefer to use 'straights', in other words individual feeds such as oats, barley, maize, hay and so on. No one, however well qualified, can possibly judge the true nutritional content of a feedstuff simply by looking at it, smelling it or even tasting it, as many horsemasters do. You can judge the quality in this way, it is true, but to know the feed content you must have it analysed. You can always try out a diet on your horse to see what the results are but this is a hit-and-miss method and you also have to wait quite some time for the results to show. Furthermore, over a period of time, deficiencies or overdoses of a particular nutrient may have a hidden, adverse effect on your horse.

ROUGHAGE

Hay is the foundation of any diet, as a tasty, nutritious roughage source is fundamental to the optimal functioning of the horse's digestive system. Hay can be replaced by hayage, forage feeds and suitable feeding straws, oat being best but barley also being acceptable. As straws are low in protein, you will probably need a protein supplement or higher-protein concentrate if using them but they are excellent when hay supplies are difficult to get.

Beware of so-called 'complete' or 'hayless' diets. These aim to give the horse all its nutrients in (usually) cube form, and are claimed to contain enough fibre to bulk the horse out and make it feel satisfied. My repeated experience is that they do not do this and that the horse is also denied the many pleasurable hours of entertainment hay gives, allowing the horse to chomp away at fibrous foods as nature intended. I find that horses on 'complete' diets develop unhappy natures and stable vices.

Good feed merchants may be able to give a feed analysis of their hay, so you can, with expert help, work out what you are feeding your horse. If not, you can get it analysed yourself, probably via your vet.

The quality of hay can be judged by nose and eye. It should smell sweet or, at the very least, of nothing, never sour, musty, like tobacco (mowburnt) or in any way unpleasant. It should be 'bouncy' with life in it, so that bales spring apart when you cut the twine, rather than 'dropping down dead'! Most important, there must be no sign of mould – white, green or black – or dust when you open and shake it out. Such hay (or straw) is not even fit for bedding and can seriously damage your horse's health by, in particular, causing COPD (Chronic Obstructive Pulmonary Disease or broken wind), an allergic condition caused by dust and fungi in the lungs. Left untreated, this condition is progressive and can put your horse completely out of action.

Do not be persuaded that soaking hay damps down the dust and mould and so makes it fit to eat. Hay that is slightly dusty *may*, in an emergency, be made suitable by soaking for four

> ## *Feedstuffs*
>
> Feeds are roughly divided into roughage/bulk feeds, concentrates and roots or succulents. *Roughage* feeds are hay and hayage, straws, forage feeds, silage and bran. *Concentrates* are straight, grain feeds such as oats, barley, maize, coarse mixes and cubes. *Succulents* include carrots, apples, turnips, mangolds, soaked sugar beet pulp and the like, plus hydroponically grown grass (see p.32).

hours to damp down the dust so that it is not inhaled, while mould spores (said to be present in all hay, even of top quality, although in small amounts) will then swell to such a size that they cannot reach the tiny air spaces in the lungs where they do so much damage, but soaking leaches nutrients out of the hay and this is not ideal.

Hayage, being moist and available in various energy grades (see p.32), is ideal for horses with breathing disorders as it is dust-free. A common complaint is that horses get through their ration too quickly when fed the recommended amount and are left with nothing to eat or do. You can get round this by feeding a hayage of lower nutritional quality but in larger amounts and also by using special small-mesh nets, so that the horse has to fiddle out a little at a time, thus eking out the ration and taking longer.

Hayage will have its nutritional analysis printed on the bale.

Hay and hayage are most conveniently fed in haynets or corner hay racks, although top studs feed

A hay net should be hung at the height of the horse's head so, when empty, it will not hang low enough for horse to catch a hoof in it. Hay nets are tied with a slip knot and it is safest to pass the free end through the loop, as shown, and tighten it so the horse cannot pull the knot undone and release the net.

them loose on the ground to prevent possible accidents to foals.

Silage is not a popular feed for horses (at least not with their owners) as it is messy and risky to feed. Transporting the large bales often results in punctured polythene covers, so that air and contamination get in and quickly become dangerous in the warm, moist environment of the silage bale. The resulting illness (botulism) has proven fatal in the past among stock who have eaten bad silage. If you can find a safe source, make the changeover from hay very gradual, over a period of several weeks. Nutritional analysis is vital, as silage can be very rich.

Hay and straw are often fed as *chop*, often incorrectly called chaff, which is cut up small and used to bulk out, and add roughage to, concentrate feeds, also encouraging the horse to chew them properly. Quality is just as important with chop, so check it before purchase. If you are ever delivered substandard feed, send it back without paying. Never risk your horse's health.

Molassed chop is coated with molasses (black treacle) and is enjoyed by most horses. Molassine meal is also a popular, sweet and tasty additive (black treacle mixed with peat!) that horses like. Molasses is also often mixed with sugar beet pulp for extra palatability.

CONCENTRATES

Oats have long been the traditional hard feed for horses. They are energy-rich and also contain a useful amount of fibre/roughage in their husks, so are easy to digest and tasty. Fed to excess, however, they cause giddiness and silly behaviour as well as producing the normal problems of feeding any concentrate in over-large amounts – possible colic, azoturia or tying up, lymphangitis and so on, as well as dull coats and itchy skin in some horses, and especially in ponies, to which oats should seldom be fed.

Oats have a high content of phytin or phytic acid, which can block the absorption of calcium in the diet (as can other grain feeds) and this can

Left: Chop – chopped-up hay and/or straw – used to add bulk and roughage to a feed. **Right:** Chop with molasses added for taste. It has a brown colour and smells sweet.

sometimes be seen, particularly in Thoroughbred youngsters, over-fed in preparation for the foal and yearling sales, with their hot, swollen joints and 'contracted tendons'. Cereal grains are generally low in calcium and high in phosphorus (hay, hayage and straw are the reverse) so bone problems can occur in animals on a high concentrate/low hay diet.

Barley suits many animals better than oats. It is not so 'intoxicating' and is generally less irritating to the digestive system and skin but is lower in fibrous husk. It is, therefore, more concentrated than oats, about 0.3 kg (¾ lb) barley approximating in feed value to 0.4 kg (1 lb) oats, so you must be sure to adjust your quantities accordingly and also add more chop to the feed.

Both oats and barley should be fed crushed, rolled or bruised (different extents of breaking open the grain to make it easier to chew and digest) but *any* grain so treated should be used

within a fortnight or it will start to rot and become unfit to feed. Oats can be fed whole but many horses do not chew them properly and they then pass through the digestive tract unused and wasted. Barley, which is too hard to feed whole, is often fed cooked and flaked, extruded or micronized – all processes aimed at increasing its digestibility.

Flaked *maize* is a popular, high-energy feed but it is low in fibre and protein, so it should be used only as part of the diet and not as a staple.

Cubes or *nuts* are commercially blended concentrate feeds available in various energy grades for different categories of animal, such as racehorse cubes (for any hard-working horses, like eventers), horse and pony cubes (for general work, such as riding club events), children's pony cubes or higher-protein cubes for breeding stock, etc. Reputable firms issue leaflets explaining which product is best for your animal and giving feeding guides, which I feel are often too generous. Cobs and ponies, in particular, are notoriously good doers and would become impossibly fat and giddy on some of the recommended rations I have seen.

An incredibly blinkered attitude, still prevalent in some horse people, is that they won't feed cubes because they can't see what is in them. Cubes are made up of various concentrate grains and other good feeds which are not commonly available to 'ordinary' horse owners but can be bought in by feed firms in quantities large enough to make them economical. They are combined with more conventional feeds and bound into cubes, nuts or pellets with syrup, honey or molasses. They are scientifically balanced and, provided they are fed correctly, are an excellent, safe feed. You should not need any supplements if you use the right grade of nut for your animal. They also have a longer storage time than other feeds, provided they are kept dry.

Coarse mixes have the same practical qualities as cubes and are also scientifically formulated and balanced in different categories. Usually molassed, or with syrup added, they are moist and do not need damping as do most 'straights', and are ideal for horses with respiratory (breathing) problems. It is easier to see what is in a coarse mix and it has the advantage of being tastier than cubes, so that horses do not 'go off' it as many do with cubes. Coarse mixes do not keep as long as cubes and should be stored in as cool a place as possible, ideally in a large, old fridge in the feed room.

With cubes and coarse mixes, all the owner has to do is feed the recommended amount of the right grade (perhaps a little less if your animal is a good doer) and you can hardly go wrong. You also have easy telephone access to the manufacturer's nutritionist if you have any queries or problems. It is not usually much use asking feed merchants for advice on nutrition.

Bran is the empty, outer husks of wheat grains that are left after the milling process. Nutritional research over the last decade or so has shown that bran is not a vital horse feed, particularly the modern product which is very expensive and low in nutritional quality. It is more effective and cheaper to use chop to provide roughage.

Bran is extremely high in phosphorus and very low in calcium, so just as with cereals, feeding too much bran can cause brittle, porous bones which are then prone to bruising, sore shins, splints, fractures, bone spavins, concussion injuries and so on.

Some authorities still recommend feeding a bran mash once a week before a rest day, or using bran mashes as a so-called laxative diet for horses that are off work or sick, the object being to replace the concentrates (which are not needed by such horses) and thus prevent over feeding the horse. Bran mashes were once said to be easy for a sick or tired horse to digest and were favoured as tempting for a jaded appetite. Nowadays, however, we know better. Fed damp and cooked (by steeping in boiling water) it does indeed act as a laxative but only because it irritates the gut and the digestive system pushes it through to get rid of it as quickly as possible. If the horse is constipated (horses have very delicate digestions, so this could, in practice, be the result of an impaction somewhere along the tract), a bran mash is unlikely to do an efficient unblocking job, probably just being squeezed past the impaction if this is possible and giving the owner the impression that all is now well. A significantly constipated horse should always receive veterinary attention.

Bran mashes also taste pretty awful (like pure bran breakfast cereals without any flavourings added to make them acceptable), so this is hardly the thing to offer a horse that needs its appetite tempting!

Finally, feeding a bran mash once a week goes directly against the well-known advice to make no sudden changes in feeding (see p. 32). Presenting the digestive micro-organisms with a sudden change like this upsets the 'balance of the bugs' and can actually cause indigestion if not painful colic.

All in all, bran is not a valuable horse food and you would do well to spend your money elsewhere. If you wish to give a 'false' feed (one with a low energy level, perhaps because a horse has suddenly been thrown out of work), try a mixture of dried grass or alfalfa (both commercially available as branded products) with soaked sugar beet pulp. This is nutritionally balanced but fairly low in energy and, as sugar beet pulp is high in calcium and low in phosphorus, it is ideal for mixing with cereals in any case. You could add molassed chop and thinly sliced roots

or simply feed these alone as your false feed.

The important thing is to make up a false feed, or any feed, using ingredients that already form part of your horse's diet. This is dealt with on p. 32, but, basically, any new feed needs introducing very gradually. You can change the *quantity* of a particular ingredient, but not the ingredients themselves, on a daily basis.

Judging the quality of concentrates depends on smell, sight and maybe taste. Reject anything that seems at all 'off', sour, musty or looks tainted or actually dirty. Cubes must be hard and dry, coarse mixes sweet and not soggy, oats, barley and maize bone-dry, free-running when you push your hand through them and smell faintly pleasant or of nothing. They should taste like what they are, or faintly nutty, if you decide to chew them.

Forage feeds have already been mentioned. Different firms produce differently formulated products which may look different. Some look like chopped up hayage, some rather like hay and some like chop itself with other herbage added. Any reputable firm's product is safe to use and forage feeds really are the most 'natural' artificial form of feed yet made available. As they become more and more popular, I feel that feeding problems in general should be reduced among the equine population. You *can* add higher protein or higher energy supplements to them, if needed, preferably from the same firm's range to maintain the balance. Some forage feeds can be fed in nets or racks, others in large mangers, the object being that they are nearly all intended to be given on a free-feed, *ad lib* basis. Follow the company's advice and you should be safe.

SUCCULENTS AND ROOTS

These are essential additions to a stabled horse's diet and very acceptable to it.

You can give carrots, turnips and mangolds (both of these last two can be left whole in the manger for the horse to crunch on overnight), eating apples, sugar beet pulp, which is available in flakes (shreds) or cubes, and fodder beets, if available. Carrots and apples should be thinly sliced or

coarsely grated to avoid any chance of the horse choking on a chunk.

Sugar beet pulp *must* be soaked in at least twice its own volume of cold water so that it swells to its maximum before being mixed with other feed. Sugar beet has the capacity (particularly in cube form) to swell inside the horse if not soaked properly and there is then a chance that it could cause a fatal impaction. It is true that ordinary horse cubes also swell considerably when soaked but these are more easily broken down and are less 'solid' than beet shreds. The time required for soaking will probably be 24 hours, particularly for the cubes which are often compacted, so don't skimp on this.

Sugar beet with molasses added (the most palatable type) should be kept cool, as should molassine meal, as it soon goes rancid and sour, so these are also excellent candidates for storing in an old fridge.

HOW MUCH SHOULD I FEED?

Before deciding this, you must learn to assess your own animal's condition and recognize, honestly, whether it is too fat, too thin or just right. For normal athletic riding or driving work, you should be able to feel the ribs fairly easily but not actually to see them.

You should feed your animal according to its bodyweight when just right in condition. If the horse is too fat, feed less and vice versa. To gauge the bodyweight, use a weighbridge if there is one near you, otherwise measure around the girth and then

Dry sugar beet shreds. They must be soaked for 24 hours in twice their own volume of cold water before they are added to feeds.

read off the likely weight according to the tables below. You can also use a special Equi-Tape, available from tack stores.

Once you know the weight, you should feed about 2.5 per cent of the bodyweight daily, (2 per cent for cobs and ponies) totalling both roughage and concentrates where both are used. This means that if your horse weighs 453.5 kg (1,000 lb) you would feed a total of 11.3 kg (25 lb) daily. For a horse in light work, this could be all good meadow hay; for medium to fairly active work of about two hours' daily recreational hacking and some schooling, you could make this three-quarters or two-thirds hay and the rest concentrates. This sort of diet is also suitable for light hunting, dressage, show jumping and so on. As the severity of the work increases,

you can reduce the roughage to about half and half.

You will often find it recommended that hard-working horses should receive only one-third, or even less of their allowance as roughage (racehorse or seed hay) but I feel this is too extreme for the equine digestive system although horses do vary in their needs and many may thrive on this ratio. Horses in very hard work could be fed 3 per cent of their bodyweight, or kept at 2.5 per cent with the addition of a cupful of corn oil or soya oil in their concentrate feed to make the feed more energy-dense.

Of course, if your horse is doing little, or no, real work, you can feed less, say, 2 per cent of the bodyweight, comprising all good hay or whatever you are using.

Bodyweight tables

Ponies and cobs

Girth (in)	40	42.5	45	47.5	50	52.5	55	57.5
Girth (cm)	101	108	114	120	127	133	140	146
Bodyweight (lb)	100	172	235	296	368	430	502	562
Bodyweight (kg)	45	77	104	132	164	192	234	252

Horses

Girth (in)	55	57.5	60	62.5	65	67.5
Girth (cm)	140	146	152	159	165	171
Bodyweight (lb)	538	613	688	776	851	926
Bodyweight (kg)	240	274	307	346	380	414

Girth (in)	70	72.5	75	77.5	80	82.5
Girth (cm)	178	184	190	199	203	206
Bodyweight (lb)	1014	1090	1165	1278	1328	1369
Bodyweight (kg)	453	486	520	570	593	611

(Based on the work of Glushanok, Rochlitz & Skay, 1981)

Hydroponic grass

This is grass that has been grown in water alone or in water with liquid nutrients added to it and it is becoming an increasingly popular method of feeding succulent fodder, of known nutritional value, to stabled horses or those without access to pasture.

Commercial units are available for large and small yards or you can rig up a very cheap one at home, using open bookshelves in a window and sowing your seed, obtainable from seed merchants or commercial marketing units, in ice-cream containers, seed trays, roasting tins, etc. Sow one shelf a day and within two weeks you will have a daily supply of juicy grass to feed to your horse, roots and all.

In winter, you may need to subject your home made unit to plant lights, bulbs that give out light from the full spectrum, unlike ordinary fluorescent or candescent bulbs, so that it gets artificial daylight like a well-lit commercial greenhouse, otherwise you may not achieve sufficient growth of grass.

ENERGY LEVELS

You should look for products which state that they contain 10–12 MJ (megajoules) of DE (digestible energy) for horses in moderate to fairly hard work. Megajoules are simply scientific measures of energy and digestible energy is the amount that the horse is able to digest from the feed – not all the food is digestible – if it were, the horse would produce no droppings. For horses in severe work, you can look for slightly higher

levels, while for those in light work or resting, and also for ponies and cobs, you want no more than 8.5–10 MJ of DE.

It is, of course, very difficult, if not impossible, to assess the amount and quality of the grass a horse eats. You will simply have to keep a close eye on the animal's behaviour and physical condition and adjust its grazing and feed accordingly.

THE GOLDEN RULES OF FEEDING

These rules have been formulated over generations and are basically good advice. The trouble is, we often do not interpret them correctly.

ʊ *Feed little and often* is the most important rule. In addition, it is wise to remember that the horse has a small stomach so that, if you are feeding concentrates, you should give no more than about 2 kg (4 lb) in one feed. Give as many frequent, small feeds per day as you can possibly manage to ensure maximum digestion.

ʊ *Water before feeding.* The thinking here is that if horses do not have water always available a large drink taken *after* food could wash undigested portions on through the digestive tract before they are ready and cause colic. Horses with water always available are unlikely to suffer from this.

ʊ *Make any changes in diet gradually.* This does not mean over days but over weeks, several if necessary. When changing from one batch of food to a new delivery, don't use up all of the old first but start mixing the two (whether hay, concentrates or whatever) two to three weeks before the existing supply is due to run out to give the digestive organisms a chance to adapt. One batch of a branded product may even differ slightly from the next. Also do this if changing from hay to hayage or introducing a new concentrate. Put in a single handful per feed for a few days and then very gradually change over, as required.

U *Use good quality feed.* The horse family has a delicate digestive system and can easily become ill if given bad food – if it is eaten at all. Horses will often go hungry before they will eat what they consider to be rubbish.

U *Do not work immediately after feeding.* This is good advice for a stabled horse that has just had a full concentrate feed. Wait an hour before working and then stick to walk for the first half hour. With horses on *ad lib* feeding systems and grass-kept horses, this is less crucial but it is still advisable to keep to walk for the first half hour. If a full stomach is lurched around by hard or fast work, it can press against the lungs, which will affect both.

U *Feed something succulent in every feed* to stabled or yarded horses to replace grass and satisfy their craving for this type of food.

U *Feed according to work, weather, constitution and temperament.* Your skill as a horsemaster comes entirely into play here!

U *Try to keep to the same feeding times each day.* This is more important for stabled horses *not* on *ad lib* systems, while for others half an hour early or late now and then is not crucial. What is important, and is a situation often overlooked, is horses missing an entire meal while out hunting or at a show and their owners thinking nothing of it. Imagine what this does to the animal's digestive system. Always try to get some feed into your horse, even if you only pack your pockets with nuts or whatever it normally has, to keep the digestive 'bugs' happy. Also, it is not a crime to let horses nibble a bit of grass during a check or a break. The small amount taken is unlikely to cause problems and the horse will feel much better for it.

U *Feed plenty of roughage.* If you bed your horse on straw and find that much of it is disappearing every night, you are obviously not feeding enough hay or whatever other roughage source you use. Feeding generous amounts of *good* hay will not result in your horse getting a 'hay belly'. It is straw and poor hay that cause this. You will rarely go wrong by giving a horse as much good hay (or whatever) as it wants and you may be pleasantly surprised to find out consequently how few concentrates it needs, if any. Conversely, generous amounts of concentrates can easily make a horse physically ill or mentally 'crazy'. If in doubt, leave them out, stick to hay or hayage and seek expert advice.

CHAPTER 4

FEET AND SHOES

The diagram below shows the basic construction of the foot, which is built around the final bone of the leg, the crescent-shaped pedal bone, which gives the foot its shape. The sides of this bone are lined with sensitive laminae or leaves (rather like the underside of a mushroom), running from top to bottom; these interlock with insensitive or horny laminae lining the inside of the hoof wall, the bond being made even firmer by means of additional 'fingers' of horn and fleshy tissue on the laminae bonding closely together. It is this bond that is entirely responsible for bearing the horse's weight. The bottom of the pedal bone does not bear any weight.

The hoof is not the hard, rigid structure it looks like from the outside, but actually flattens and expands slightly each time the horse puts weight on it, contracting again when the weight is removed. This acts as a pumping mechanism, maintaining the health and the integrity of the tissue of the feet and legs. The sensitive, fleshy tissues of the feet are rich in blood, contained in a network of fine blood vessels called capillaries. As the foot is squashed under the horse's weight, the capillaries are flattened and the blood is pushed into the veins running up the leg, which have valves in them to prevent the blood running back down as the weight is

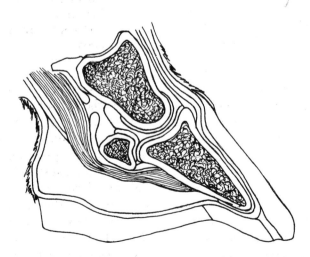

This cross-section of the foot shows the natural angulation of the pedal bone which may become loosened in laminitis.

released. This action creates capacity within the capillaries for fresh blood, which is drawn in from the arteries, carrying oxygen and nutrients needed by the living tissue. Waste products are carried away in the blood going up the veins.

This pumping mechanism is vital to the health of the foot and leg, and also acts to reduce concussion considerably. The old theory of the frog being the anti-concussion feature thus needs to be expanded. In a newly shod foot, the frog cannot touch the ground; horses who do little but roadwork may not suffer from concussion as it is the whole foot that is involved.

The absorption of concussion is assisted by the angle of the pasterns, the slightly elastic quality of the tendons and, to a lesser extent, ligaments. As weight is put on the foot, the pastern sinks down, softening the blow, then the slight elastic recoil in the tendons helps the leg to spring back up again (sending the horse onward in its gait) with no energy used. Another energy-saving feature, also contributing to the horse's stamina, is that there are no muscles below the knees and hocks but only in the upper legs (and also in the shoulders and hips, of course). This means that the lower legs and feet are light to move, requiring less energy and effort from the muscles.

SHOEING

For horses that work on hard surfaces, shoeing is necessary to prevent wear occurring faster than it can be replaced. Most horses and ponies are still shod with metal shoes and nails,

Laminitis

In the extremely painful and distressing disease of laminitis, the bond becomes loosened due to failure of tissue strength because of an impaired blood supply. If the disease progresses, the pedal bone becames detached from the inside of the wall, starting at the toe, and starts to sink down. Because the bone is naturally angled downwards at the toe, the toe area of the bone may penetrate the sensitive, or even the insensitive, sole. According to research done by Robert Eustace, FRCVS, of the Laminitis Clinic at Mead House Farm, Dauntsey, in England, it does not actually rotate, but may give the impression of having done so because of its natural angulation within the foot.

The main cause of laminitis is over-feeding and it is therefore often due to bad management but there are other causes such as trauma, possibly due to concussion, blood poisoning, or any condition that alters the chemical balance of the blood or interferes with its circulation.

although synthetic shoes, sometimes part-synthetic, part-metal, and sometimes incorporating nails, sometimes adhesives, are also now increasing. They *are* more expensive but claim to, and seem in practice to, help to reduce the concussion transmitted up the leg with each step.

When a farrier shoes a horse, he should first observe how it moves, then study the wear on both the bearing surface (the surface touching the horse's hoof) and the ground

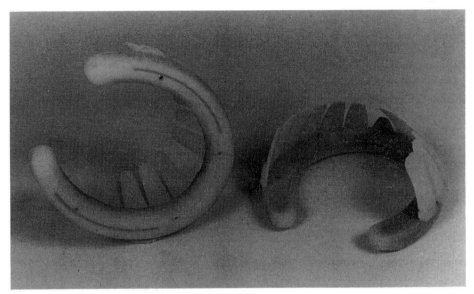

This type of synthetic shoe is glued to the foot. These are used mainly for veterinary purposes or when a horse will not tolerate nailing on. There are several different types, all useful.

surface of the shoe. The shoe always moves very slightly on the foot and the metal will be worn smooth on the bearing surface, indicating to the farrier where, perhaps, weight has been unevenly borne.

The farrier can either make the shoes entirely from scratch from a bar of mild steel or, as is most common these days, alter ready-made, bought-in shoes after heating the metal in his forge. The shoe is tried against the hoof while the metal is hot, to check the evenness of the bearing surface, the shoe being carried to the foot by means of a special rod called a pritchel, which is inserted into one of the nail holes.

Hot shoeing has advantages and disadvantages. It does allow for an exact fit, the shoe always being made to fit the foot rather than the foot being cut about to fit the shoe, except in cases where, say, a deformed foot is

being encouraged to grow into a more normal shape at the discretion of the vet and farrier. Cold metal can be altered to some extent but not so exactly. Placing hot metal against horn, however, does cause some horn shrinkage. Later, when the hoof becomes wet at some point after shoeing, it will expand slightly, making the shoes very slightly too small.

Some farriers tend to burn on the shoe too much, not only causing significant shrinkage but also burning away the horn to fit a shoe that is not quite correct for the foot. Dense clouds of acrid smoke are the give away here! 'Burning a bed for the shoe' (as the excuse goes) is not only unnecessary but harmful.

Some horses are frightened by the hiss and smell that accompanies hot shoeing and for these (as with most racehorses) cold shoeing can be

Below: *A commonly-used fore hunter shoe. The ground surface is grooved to take the nail heads and to make the shoe lighter and reduce suction in mud. The inside edge is also concaved out from the sole for similar reasons, making the bearing surface which touches the hoof wider than the ground surface. The heels are tapered to minimize treads and suction.*

Below: *A hind shoe with holes in the heels to take studs of various types.*

Below: *It is generally best for the foot to be balanced so that, when seen from the front, the ends of the coronet are the same height from the ground. This helps to ensure even distribution of weight up and down the centre of the foot and leg.*

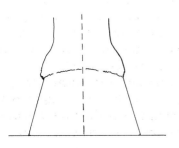

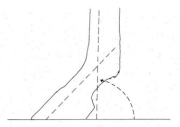

Above: *From the side, the hoof wall at the toe and the long pastern bone should run upwards at the same angle in a continuous line. The angle the forefeet make with the ground should be about 45°. The hind feet and pasterns are usually a little more upright.*

Above: *In a well-shod foot the nail holes will be the same height all round unless the farrier is avoiding cracks or chips. The shoes are taken well back to support the heels and the toe will be slightly rolled or knocked under to assist the natural action and make the horse more comfortable. In a newly-shod foot it is extremely unlikely that the frog will touch hard ground.*

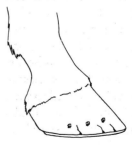

Above: *In a foot that need shoeing the horn may be growing over the shoe or may be cracking upwards from the ground surface and the clenches (the turned-up tops of the nails gripping the shoe) will be loosened and have risen up in their holes. The shoe may be loose.*

excellent. A useful in-between method is to shape the shoe hot, cool it down (by plunging it into cold water), try it on the foot, then heat it up again to alter it. Unfortunately, few farriers seem to do this.

The nail holes in a shoe are in the front half of it. This is to allow that vital expansion of the foot, which mostly takes place in the back half of the foot. A foot held tightly together by nails cannot expand sufficiently, so the farrier must draw a fine line between positioning the nails to keep the shoe on and allowing the foot to expand.

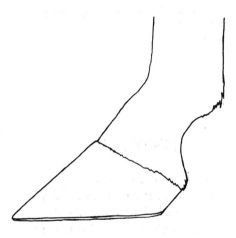

A common, faulty way to shoe a horse is to leave the shoe heels too short for the foot and to rasp the heels down too far and the toes not far enough. The correct angle seen on the previous page is lost, correct foot balance is destroyed and the foot and leg subjected to stress and strain and probable eventual injury and/or laminitis.

When shoeing is over, the shoe should come right out to the edges of the walls of the foot (unless the farrier has 'feathered' the shoes, tapering them in on the inside branches for a horse that hits itself) and, *most important*, the branches of the shoes should fit well back at the heels to provide sufficient support. A failure to do this, plus allowing the toes to remain too long, will gradually deform the foot and undermine its strength and that of the leg. Over a period of months or years, this can cause mechanical laminitis as the inner structure of the foot is put under unnatural distorting stresses and the laminae are very gradually forced apart.

GOING BAREFOOT

Horses and ponies working mainly on soft surfaces, with some work on *smooth*, hard surfaces, such as smooth, as opposed to gritted, tarmac, can often work successfully without shoes. They need good basic foot conformation, even wear, straight action, good natural horn quality and a correct, balanced diet to maintain sound horn growth. It is also best if they have naturally arching soles as flat feet are more susceptible to bruising and pressure, the soles not being intended to bear much, if any, weight.

You will still need the services of a good farrier for periodic checks and trimming to maintain foot balance and to keep an expert eye on the feet, particularly round the edges where the horn can chip and crack, and also at the white line. This is a region of pale, softer horn, indicating where the sensitive and insensitive laminae meet inside the foot, and tiny pebbles can become embedded here, causing problems. Sandy surfaces can also cause wear here. Occasionally, a tiny

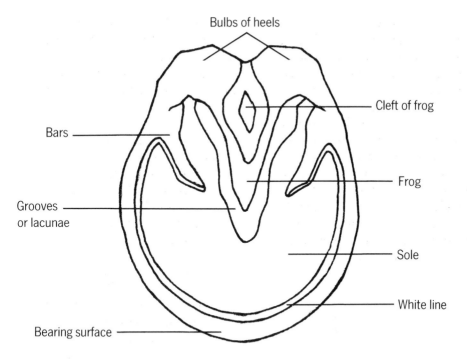

Bulbs of heels

Cleft of frog

Bars

Frog

Grooves
or lacunae

Sole

White line

Bearing surface

The ground surface of the horse's hoof.

stone may even work its way in and travel up to the coronet at the top of the hoof (where the horn is made) allowing an infection to develop (this can happen in shod horses, too).

It is a good plan to discuss with your farrier the prospects of your horse working successfully without shoes. Most good farriers are so hard-worked that I'm sure you won't get any complaints about loss of business! A master farrier once said to me: 'The best shoe is no shoe'. Any good farrier will agree that, whether temporary or permanent, a period without shoes allows the foot to work completely naturally, which is good for it. It is also noticeable that most feet increase by at least one size after a few weeks without shoes.

DAILY FOOT CARE

The importance of regular foot care is often underestimated. Each day you should check that your horse is moving freely and straight, noting whether any natural irregularities in its action are getting worse – or even better. Feel the temperature of the feet with the backs of your fingers, which are more sensitive than the insides. Any heat should worry you. Although heat is not necessarily a sign of laminitis, which is usually due to too little blood circulating in the feet rather than too much, it could signify some other problem.

With your finger, feel around the top of the coronet firmly. If you detect any sign of a 'ditch' here,

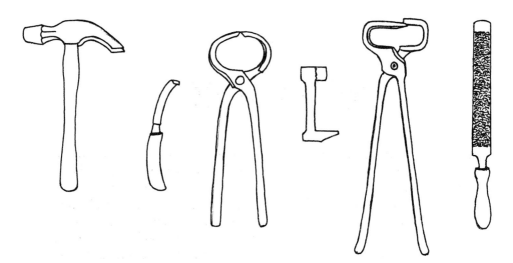

Farrier's tools. From the left: *hammer, drawing knife for trimming, pincers for levering off the shoe, buffer for cutting clenches to remove the shoe and – with the hammer – for cutting off horn, hoof cutters for cutting off excess horn, and rasp for smoothing horn and removing excess growth.*

either at the front or, more seriously, all round, it is probably a sign that your animal has chronic, if slight, laminitis and the pedal bone is detaching. Amazing though it may sound, owners and farriers can easily miss this gradual onset in an animal they know well.

Also check the condition of the horn and the state of the shoes, and gently try to fit the end of a hoofpick under the heels of the shoes and move them. If you can, the shoes are loose.

Pick out the feet twice daily or more if needed. Work firmly but gently from toe to heel in order not to push grit under the shoes at the heels. Poke out all mud, manure and debris. Work thoroughly in the lacunae (grooves) at the sides of the frog (see diagram) and in the cleft of the frog, without being rough, as the horse can easily feel what you are doing here. It is the farrier's job to remove excess

horn from the frog, which may overgrow the cleft and lacunae, allowing infection to develop underneath. Press the back of the hoofpick against the frog, particularly towards the rear, and note any sensitivity, such as the horse flinching or pulling its foot away, as this could be a sign of soreness and infection.

There is no need to wash your horse's feet nor to oil them daily. Many hoof dressings do no good and can even hamper the permeability of the horn. If a hoof conditioner is needed, seek advice from your vet or a really good farrier as those that actually benefit the horn and can be absorbed are few and far between.

Hoof hardeners or conditioners may be bought to toughen up poor horn and enable a horse to work barefoot. If you fancy using one of these, discuss their qualities and benefits with your vet or farrier.

CHAPTER 5

BEDDING

Horses are more fortunate than most farm animals in that they are normally still stabled on some form of bedding material that is kept fairly clean and plentiful.

ZERO-BEDDING SYSTEMS FOR HORSES

Various flooring materials and tiles are now sold for use in stables, aimed at enabling horses and their owners to do away with bedding. They all are porous, allowing urine to drain through to the floor below. The floor must be well drained and slope slightly towards an outlet or perhaps a centre drain, otherwise the object is defeated and the floor beneath will be swimming in urine. The materials are all intended to provide a warm material for the horse to lie on, as well as remaining dry. You can always put a little bedding on top, if you wish, particularly when introducing a horse to the new system. Some horses take to it well, others obviously prefer bedding.

REASONS FOR BEDDING

We provide bedding to cushion and protect the horse when it lies down or rolls, to provide warmth and protection from ground draughts and also for comfort. Horses that feel warm and comfortable and secure underfoot (vital to an animal whose survival depends on four sound legs and feet to flee from danger) thrive better mentally and physically than others, often requiring less food to remain in good condition. They are more settled and contented and work better.

DRAINAGE FLOORINGS

Stable floors made of concrete are cold, hard and absorbent, effectively

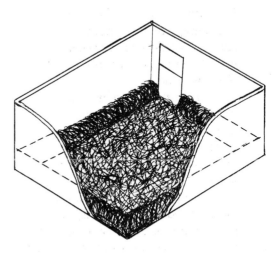

A well-made straw bed should have a really generous banking round the sides for warmth and to act as a cushion. The middle of the bed should be sufficiently thick so that the hardness of the floor cannot be felt beneath your feet. There should not be an empty space behind the door.

soaking up urine as well as water. Old-fashioned, hard stable bricks are very hard-wearing (particularly the blue ones) but also very expensive, whereas concrete is probably the cheapest material around. The bricks have drainage channels in them to carry the urine, whereas concrete floors usually have a herringbone pattern of drainage grooves sloping slightly to an outlet and drain. A sloping floor is obviously necessary but these grooves are a waste of time as the urine will largely be soaked up by the bedding.

Some stables have earth floors on which you lay the bedding directly. The urine drains straight through and this systems works well in practice although some local authorities do not permit them.

House bricks, in Britain, particularly hard, red Accrington bricks, laid on their sides about 1 cm apart, with the gaps filled with fine gravel make a good flooring through which urine will drain. It is best to lay the bricks on an excavated bed of gravel and rammed rubble to maintain evenness.

Wood should never be used for stable flooring as, not only does it absorb urine, it also rots and becomes slippery when wet.

My favourite drainage flooring is loose-weave asphalt laid over gravel on top of rubble in an excavated bed. The trick is *not* to tamp down the asphalt, as is normal, as this closes up the essential holes between the little lumps, through which the urine will drain and which are the whole purpose of the floor. The most that should be done is a very light smoothing off to make it even.

BEDDING MATERIALS

The most common beds are of straw or wood shavings. Shredded paper and sawdust also make good bedding. From time to time, other patented, usually synthetic, materials appear on the market.

If properly managed, *straw* makes a warm, springy, resilient, comfortable bed, suitable for any system, whether full mucking-out, semi deep-litter or full deep-litter. Nowadays, more and more people are becoming aware of the advantages of keeping their animals on what is known as a clean-air regime, which means an environment as free from stable dust and moulds as possible. Dust and moulds are known to favour the development of respiratory diseases and allergies and, unfortunately, all hay and straw, even when of top quality, contain *some* level of them. Ordinary straw is therefore not suitable for a clean-air regime or for animals that are susceptible to respiratory disorders. However, vacuum-cleaned straw is now available, as are straw-cleaning machines, which are only suitable for large yards.

Shavings make a fair bedding material, if not quite as easy to handle as straw. They are not as warm as straw, nor as cheap as they used to be, but are less dusty. Ordinary shavings do contain some dust, however, but, here again, you can buy dust-extracted shavings. Unfortunately, EC rules now demand that growing trees are sprayed with certain chemicals, the residues of which can stay on the shavings and, ultimately, come into contact with your horse which may develop a skin or hoof problem as a result! Although not yet a widespread problem, this is something to watch for.

Most people allow shavings beds to remain too damp. Urine (and spilled water) spread and soak easily into shavings and to keep a shavings bed really dry you would need to remove most of it daily. A layer of dampish shavings on the floor underneath the clean ones does provide some stability, shavings being notorious for scattering easily and exposing the floor. Shavings are normally used on a semi deep-litter system.

Shredded paper is an excellent bedding once you have learned the knack of managing it. It is sold as being as dust-free and sterile as it is practically possible to get and is excellent for horses with respiratory problems. It is used on a semi deep-litter system. It makes a warm, springy, comfortable bedding (much more so than shavings) and horses like it. Very absorbent, shredded paper dries out quickly when tossed and aired.

Sawdust is not widely used but, if used generously and, like any other bedding, managed properly, it makes a very good bed. Contrary to popular opinion, it does not heat up and become maggoty. It is warmer than shavings but not as warm as straw or paper.

A perfectly dreadful bedding material in my experience, is *peat*. Whether you use sedge peat or sphagnum moss peat, it is *extremely* absorbent and slow to dry out. It is dusty and impossible to vacuum clean, of course, and makes a cold, irritating, damp bed.

Mucking out tools. *At the back, from the left:* yard broom, shovel and dung skep. *At the front, from the left:* dung scoop and rake for removing droppings from the paddock, and shavings rake used for picking up droppings from a shavings bed.

BEDDING SYSTEMS

In *full mucking-out*, you remove the droppings and all the wet material once daily. In between times, you 'skep out' (remove droppings either in a proper dung skep [pronounced 'skip'] or in a substitute such as a dustbin lid) and remove any very dirty, wet bedding and fluff up the bedding or add new material at night, called 'setting fair'.

This system lends itself to straw and people who have a lot of time. The quickest way to muck out a straw bed fully is first to remove all droppings with a shovel, feeling around with your feet for hidden piles. Tip them into a wheelbarrow or muck sack in the open stable doorway (having previously, ideally, temporarily removed the horse). Sort out the cleanest corner of the box and fork the clean straw into it. Next fork the semi-clean stuff into another corner so that you are left with only wet, dirty material, which you then shovel into the barrow.

Now scrape stubborn dirt off the floor with the back of the shovel, brush the floor firmly and, ideally, hose it down. Leave the bedding up to air and dry the floor, preferably while the horse is at exercise or turned out.

To bed down, take your semi-clean material and spread it, criss-cross fashion, over the floor. Do the same with the clean stuff over the top of it and finally bring in new straw, thoroughly shaken out, to make up the thickness of the bed and to bank all round the sides of the box so that the finished bed looks as much like the inside of a bird's nest as possible! Mean little banks do not bounce the horse back if it lies too close to the wall where it will be in danger of getting cast, nor do they protect it against floor draughts. Do not leave a bare space behind the door, a practice beloved by those who cannot bear to see a bit of bedding on the yard. Horses stand here for long periods looking out, and it is kinder and better for them to have bedding to stand on. Whenever you leave the box, kick some straw into place behind you so that any draught coming under the door is dealt with.

To skep out, simply shovel droppings and very wet bedding into the skep, pulling some clean stuff in

from the sides to make up the deficiency. Set fair at night with your fork, fluffing up the bedding and removing any droppings.

It takes a good half hour to muck out a straw bed properly – if you are fit and used to it.

Semi deep-litter is much quicker to deal with. Here, you shovel out all droppings and the worst of the bedding daily, bringing in clean stuff from the sides and adding new as needed, usually at night. You should skep out as often per day as you can. The bed is not disturbed any more, so the floor is not swept or hosed. Many working owners use semi-deep litter during the week, mucking out fully at weekends. This system is suitable for any bedding material.

Full deep-litter is also suitable for any material other than shredded paper, and can be carried on for months. Ostensibly, you just remove droppings and add new bedding on top, not disturbing the rest at all and if this sounds unbelievably filthy, be assured that, in practice and in a well-ventilated, well-drained stable, it can work very well.

The theory is that the dirty bedding at the bottom of the deep bed gradually rots down and the bed sinks, therefore the horse does not actually become in danger of hitting its head on the ceiling as you add new bedding on top. You must be absolutely scrupulous about removing droppings and, for this reason, I feel it is not really suitable for owners who are not available for long periods to skep out. You will also find it works less well in summer as it can become smelly and too warm in hot weather, allowing bacteria to breed.

Managing muck

You'll hear lots of old wives' tales about muck heaps – about how they need stamping on, combing with a fork, beating into a square, steaming brick, etc., so that they will rot down and show people that you know how to manage a yard. In practice, unless you are a real lady or gentleman of leisure, you will not have time to do all this, particularly if it is at the expense of the horse itself.

The truth is that the muck heap will rot down anyway, even if you actively try to stop it, because it is bacteria-rich organic material. Plant nurseries, who often collect muck these days, usually want fresh muck, not well-rotted stuff, and time spent beating and tidying up the muck heap is far, far better spent exercising or just being with your horse. When it comes to horse/human relationships, there is nothing more valuable than a deep affection, respect and mutual rapport between horse and owner and you will not develop this by looking after the muck heap or sweeping the yard. Keep them *reasonably* tidy, then forget them and concentrate on the horse.

Do site your muck heap downwind from the yard and house. If you live in an urban area, unless a nursery will remove the muck weekly, muck out straight into heavyweight plastic sacks and seal them with sticky tape, selling them as ready-packed manure. This will prevent complaints from your neighbours.

The main thing with any bedding is to keep it as clean as possible, whatever system or material you use. Take out droppings as thoroughly and frequently as you can. Remember that urine and rotting organic material give off noxious fumes, not least of which is ammonia, which is a severe irritant to mucous membranes and can cause respiratory problems and sore eyes, not to mention rotten feet.

To test whether your bedding is successful, walk into your box when the horse has been in for several hours and you have just spent some time outdoors, and take a slow, deep breath. If you can detect anything much other than fresh air, it's not working properly. Sit on the bed and read, meditate or whatever for half an hour and note whether you can feel damp creeping through your clothing. If you can, so can the horse and, again, the bed is not working or being managed properly. The remedy is then up to you.

Briefly, the secret of successful bedding is to ask yourself one question: 'Would I like to roll around on this and sleep in it?' If the answer is 'No', then neither would your horse. Horses are fastidious. Just like us, they want a clean, dry bed to lie on.

CHAPTER 6

SKIN AND COAT

A sleek, clean, glossy coat, which moves easily over the ribs and gleams with wellbeing, is not just a sign that someone has been busy with a brush, but that the horse is in good physical, and probably mental, health.

The skin and coat have several functions. The skin acts as an elastic, protective covering for the body beneath. It contains nerve endings which tell the horse whether it is experiencing pressure, pleasure, pain, heat or cold. It also contains sweat glands and oil glands, which work to dispel heat and which lubricate the skin and coat, helping to retain elasticity and give a degree of water-resistance. It carries tiny blood vessels which carry heat-containing blood close to the surface of the body and can thus help to cool the horse down or retain body heat. Skin also contains the hair follicles or roots and the protective colouring pigment, melanin. Areas of skin that contain no melanin, appearing pink as opposed to chocolate or black, are less resistant to water, disease, sunlight, abuse from insects, chemicals and so on. Without a healthy skin the horse's wellbeing is seriously comprised.

The coat's health depends on the skin from which it grows. Although it is composed of dead material, it plays a vital role in protecting the horse. It is, of course, shorter and finer in summer when an insulating layer of warm air next to the skin is less important and easy heat loss is needed. In winter, depending on the breed of horse, the coat can become positively furry and, although it is not actually waterproof, it gives some protection from winter weather.

SKIN CARE

Wild and feral equidae are obviously never groomed by people and yet their skin remains healthy even if it looks dirty to us. The 'dirt' is mainly dead skin scales (the skin is constantly shedding dead flakes and being replaced by new cells from the underneath layer) and natural oil (sebum) plus grains of earth picked up when the horse rolls.

Natural, mutual grooming helps to bond friends and relatives in the wild and is much appreciated among domesticated horses too. Rolling is important as it coats the horse with dust or mud which repels skin parasites. Mud hardens on to protect the horse against wind. Horses often queue up to use the same rolling patch and it is believed that this helps to coat them all with the herd smell. The coating of dust and mud also helps to remove excess grease from the coat.

In addition, horses rub themselves against tree trunks, fences or

Coat growth patterns

The horse changes its coat twice a year, gradually, shedding a little of the old coat, then growing a little of the new, several times, until, over a period of a few weeks, a complete change has taken place, apart from mane and tail hair. Coat change is stimulated by the lengthening or shortening of the daylight, which is registered by the brain. The brain then sends out hormonal signals to the body, which bring about a coat change in spring and autumn.

The coat grows back and down from the head, with various swirls, feathers, partings and so on, aimed at directing water off the body.

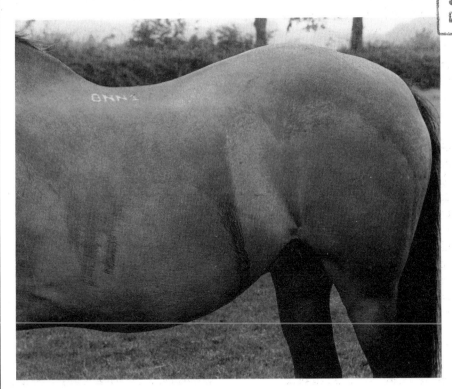

The horse's coat grows in different directions to help drain water off effectively.

whatever is handy, so they certainly do look after their own skin.

Domesticated horses at grass are fairly close to nature as regards skin care. They are rained on, they roll, mutually groom, scratch, run and so on, and their skins normally stay healthy unless attacked by disease, insects or parasites. Their coats may look sleek and glossy and it is only when you lift the hair that you see what you might call dirt.

It is commonly said that you ought not to body brush horses at grass as they need the grease in their coats to help to protect them, and this is true to some extent. However, no harm will come from giving a grass-kept horse a light body brushing before some special event, or from shampooing its mane and tail.

Shampooing stabled horses is very common these days but I feel it is often overdone. The use of soap or detergent, however mild, too often dries out the coat and promotes a dry, itchy, uncomfortable skin, prone to attack by disease and insects. Unless a horse is exceptionally dirty, or has a very greasy coat, you can get it clean enough with warm, clear water. A horse's coat is often beautifully silky

after rain alone, so go easy on the shampoo and make sure it is thoroughly rinsed out.

Of course, a refreshing hose-down on a hot day will be much appreciated by a horse once it has become used to it: remember, it is not a natural practice for wild horses to wet themselves purposely unless they cross a river. Many do, however, develop a liking for splashing themselves with water and even rolling in shallow water.

GROOMING

Grooming is time-consuming, hard work but the fitter you become the easier and quicker you'll do it. It takes about 30–45 minutes to groom a

Horses often groom each other along the back, most often around the withers. This mutual grooming is an important social bonding activity and a sign of affection and friendship.

horse thoroughly. It is also much easier to clean a fit, regularly groomed horse than one whose skin is not toned up or regularly groomed. Grooming is usually stepped up when a horse is on a fitness programme or in work but it does not, in itself, get the horse fit – only exercise and appropriate feeding do that. However, because the skin plays an important role in the excretion of metabolic toxins (waste products that are produced in greater quantities in response to extra work and feeding), it is important to keep it clean.

However, it should be said that perhaps grooming has been granted a degree of overimportance in equine theory, perhaps because it results in a good appearance, something with which so many traditionalists seem very preoccupied. You can clean a horse just as effectively by sponging or hosing down quickly with warm water. In fact, this is *more* effective than body brushing. You simply have to make sure that the horse is thoroughly dried off afterwards if the weather is at all chilly. On the rare occasions you do use shampoo, you must make absolutely sure all trace of it is rinsed from the coat.

When grooming, work out the order in which you will do everything so that nothing is forgotten. I like to begin with the feet. Use a hoofpick firmly but carefully, poking out dirt as described on p.40 and checking the feet and shoes. Next, take a *dandy*

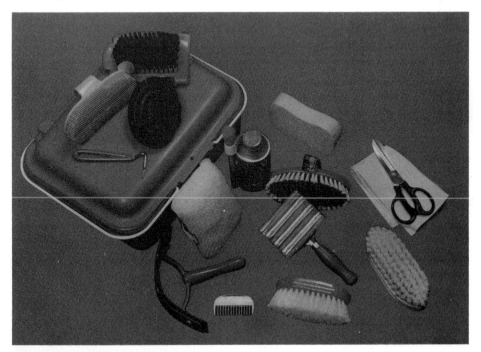

Grooming kit. On top of the container or tidy (*left to right from the back*): grooming mitt, plastic curry, rubber curry, hoof pick. On the floor (*left to right from the back*): sponge, hoof oil and brush, body brush, rubber with scissors, 'polishing' pad, metal curry comb, sweat scraper, mane comb, water brush, dandy brush.

brush and brush off all dried manure, mud, bedding and other debris. Don't be rough with the dandy brush or you will create resentment in your horse, particularly if it is tied up and feels defenceless. If you are careful and very gentle, you can even use the dandy brush to brush the mane and tail and to remove bedding from them, although you can also use your fingers for this. Roll long strands of hair between your fingers or palms to break down hardened mud, and use your fingertips to remove mud from the horse's head if it dislikes being brushed here.

The most effective way to use the *body brush* is to keep your arm slightly bent and lean your weight on it, having first placed it carefully on the coat rather then slapping it down on the horse. Pushing with your arm and shoulder muscles is very tiring. Brush firmly in long, sweeping strokes (where the body allows), making about six strokes in one place. Every two or three strokes, draw the metal curry comb across the bristles to clean them.

You don't *have* to use your left hand for the left side of the horse and vice versa. This could result in you becoming too tired to finish off one side properly! Just swap about as you wish, although, as you get fitter, you will find that it is, indeed, easier to brush that way.

The parts most often skimped when body brushing are beneath the jaw, under the forelock and mane, inside ears, behind pasterns, inside forearms and thighs and between buttocks, so don't let yourself be guilty of this. Body brush the forelock, mane and tail and, finally,

use your sponges to damp-sponge the eyes, nostrils and lips with one and the sheath or udder, and dock (between the buttocks and under the tail itself) with the other. Never mix up your sponges! How would you like it?

That describes a good, basic grooming. You can also 'lay' (damp down) the mane and tail hair with the water brush to encourage them to lie flat and many people then apply a tail bandage for the same purpose. A final dusting over with a slightly damp stable rubber gives a last polish. It is easiest and most effective to groom a horse after work when it is dry but still warm and the skin is most receptive to being cleaned.

QUARTERING

The basic tidy-up given before exercise is called quartering. Here, you simply throw the rugs back and forwards (if worn) so that you can get at the horse's four quarters (hence the name). You remove dried stable stains (manure and urine), mud and dried sweat from the coat, bedding from mane and tail, pick out feet and damp sponge both ends. This is also suitable for a stabled horse on the odd day when you just haven't time to give a thorough body brushing. It is not a sin to omit this occasionally and won't significantly affect the horse. In fact, if you hose it down, there's no point in body brushing as well.

It's true that body brushing does stimulate the skin and the act of grooming creates a bond between horse and groom if sensitively done (and the reverse if it isn't) but grooming is not as important as feeding, watering and exercising when it comes to the horse's health.

CLIPPING

Clipping is done in winter to enable the horse to work hard and to sweat without suffering the chilling effects of a long, thick wet coat, or of over-sweating and losing condition, but many horses are overclipped. There are many different clips or you can invent your own to suit your horse. The important thing is to remove only as much as is necessary and to concentrate on those areas that sweat most – the breast, neck and shoulders, followed by the belly and around the tops of the legs.

Unfortunately people often clip for appearance rather than wellbeing. *Very* few horses need a *full* or *hunter clip* unless they are working exceptionally hard or have very thick, greasy coats which are impossible to keep clean otherwise. A hunter clip is most inappropriate for a hunter, in fact, as it removes the hair from the top part of the horse, the very part that needs protection when the horse is hanging around during a check.

A *blanket clip* is suitable for any horse and you can pare this down further by just leaving the hair on the back, loins and quarters, clipping the whole body in front of the saddle.

A *trace clip* or an *Irish clip* are suitable for animals with very fine

Full clip

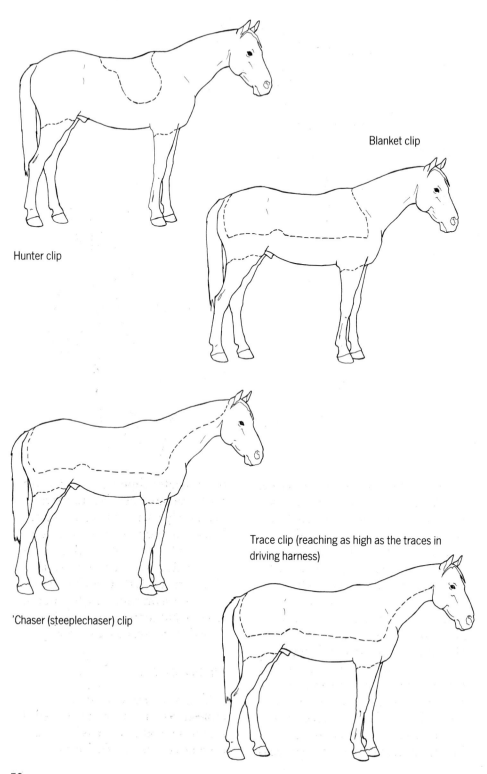

Blanket clip

Hunter clip

Trace clip (reaching as high as the traces in driving harness)

'Chaser (steeplechaser) clip

Irish clip

Breast 'n gullet clip

coats or not in hard work, the *'chaser clip* also being a smart, useful clip for working horses. One 'unofficial' but very useful clip is what I call the *'breast 'n gullet clip'*, ideal for children's ponies, working owners' hacks during winter or even fine-coated hunters in light work.

It's barely worth a one- or two-horse owner buying their own clippers. You might as well pay a professional to do a neat, stylish job. Present your horse as clean and dry as possible, provide plenty of haynets to keep it busy and rugs to cover it up gradually as clipping progresses. People always say you should increase

the feed after clipping to help to keep the horse warm but this should not necessarily refer to the concentrates. Make sure the hay or hayage is of a good grade and in plentiful supply as it is the slow, constant eating and digestion of this that will keep the horse warm on winter nights, not the sudden, but soon-played-out, boost provided by extra concentrates.

TRIMMING

Trimming can be done by a professional but, as the tools needed are cheap, you can just as easily learn (perhaps by means of an initial

To pull the mane, backcomb up to the roots so you are left with the ends of the longest hairs in one hand, then press the hairs near the roots against the mane comb with the thumb of your other hand and quickly snatch them out from the roots. Do a few hairs a day to avoid making the crest of the horse's neck sore.

lesson) to do this yourself. Even if your horse is not clipped, a neat trimming job can make a world of difference to its appearance.

Pulling and otherwise trimming the mane and tail are illustrated on this page. In addition, use scissors and comb to trim off long hairs under the jaw (rather than hand clippers which give an amateurish, shaved effect) and around the fetlocks and coronets, but leave a little frond on the ergot to assist drainage and prevent an over-trimmed look.

A neatly trimmed head will enhance your horse's appearance but I hope you will not be persuaded to clip off the antennae whiskers around the muzzle. These are part of the horse's sensory equipment: they help it to find its way and feed in the dark and when rooting in undergrowth or

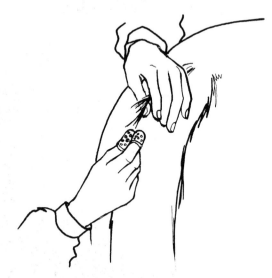

To pull the tail, use either a mane comb or rubber thimbles. Quickly pull three or four hairs out from the roots to about two-thirds down the dock, to give a tapered effect. For horses that are out a great deal it is kinder to leave the tail full and plait it for special occasions.

To trim excess hair from fetlocks, comb the hair upwards against its direction of growth and snip off the hair protruding between the teeth of the comb.

bedding and some horses will become insecure and go off their feed when they are first removed, although they adapt eventually. I always feel sorry for horses whose owners clip them off as it is such an unkind and unnecessary thing to do.

Trimming the long, tufty hair from outside the ears, particularly at the base, adds to a horse's appearance without doing any harm but you should never trim the hair from the insides of the ears as this prevents bits from falling down inside and helps to protect against cold weather. You can easily body brush inside the ears to remove grease.

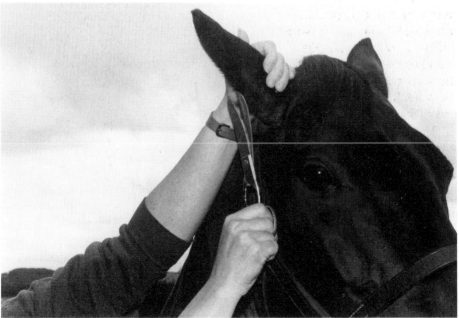

When trimming excess hair from outside the ears, gently close the edges of the ears together and carefully snip off the hair that protrudes.

55

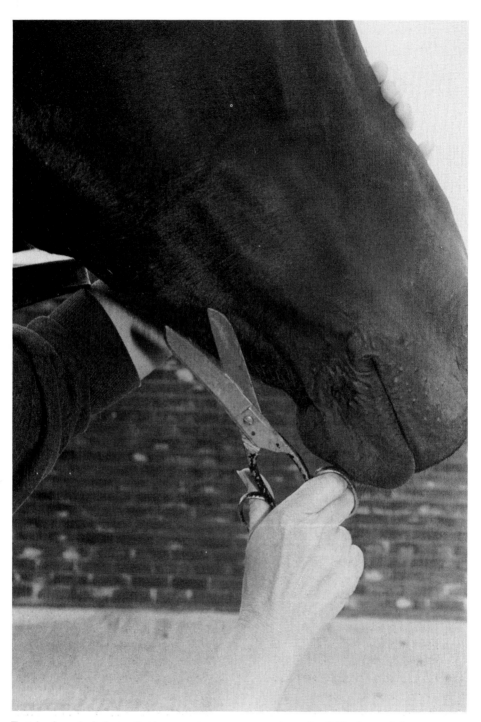

To trim long hair from the jaw, you can use a comb, as for fetlocks, or trim carefully with scissors only. In all cases, scissors give a much more professional and sympathetic look than clippers.

CHAPTER 7

TACK AND CLOTHING

This is a very large subject and I can only cover the most basic, essential items here.

THE SADDLE AND ATTACHMENTS

The most useful saddle for general riding is the general purpose saddle, also sometimes called a cross country or event saddle. This is styled so as to allow for a variable leg length according to whether you are doing flatwork or jumping: the shorter your stirrup, the further forward your knee comes and the further forward the saddle flap, and the panel underneath, need to be cut.

Buy a saddle with a spring tree rather than a rigid one. The tree is the framework on which the saddle is made. Those with metal strips or 'springs' running from pommel to cantle are called spring trees and are much more comfortable than the, now rarer, rigid tree.

Unless you are experienced and knowledgeable, always buy your saddle, and other tack and clothing, from a reputable saddler.

You will need *stirrups and stirrup leathers* of course, and it is best to buy stainless-steel stirrup irons (plain English hunting irons being the most common and practical) and buffalo-hide stirrup leathers, which are virtually unbreakable. On the inside at the bottom between the two branches your stirrup irons should be about 2 cm (1 in) wider than the widest part of your boot, for safety reasons, otherwise your foot might slip right through or get jammed; in either case you could get stuck and be dragged, should you have an accident, sustaining very serious injuries.

Two excellent types of *girth* are the Balding and the Atherstone, both of which are shaped away from the horse's elbow and so are comfortable and less likely to pinch the thin skin here. Leather girths are fine if kept clean and soft; natural fabrics must also be kept clean and soft and have the advantage of being absorbent. Synthetic, permeable fabrics, which allow sweat to be drawn away from the horse, so keeping the area drier, are fine. Non-absorbent synthetic fabrics, such as nylon, should be avoided as not only are they not absorbent, they can be rough on the skin, too.

Numnahs, saddle pads or *cloths* are a good idea if they absorb sweat (quilted cotton is excellent) or are permeable, helping to keep the back

Showing saddle with very flat seat and straight flap

General purpose/event or cross country saddle

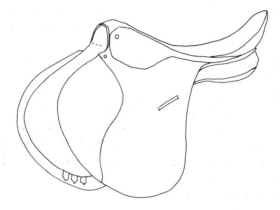

Endurance saddle with plenty of padding and moderately forward-cut flap

Dressage saddle

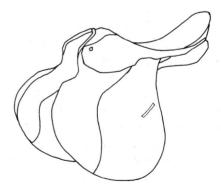

Jumping saddle used mainly for show jumping

drier and more comfortable. Avoid things such as foam-filled nylon like the plague! Acrylic fleece is fine if it is kept clean and soft.

BRIDLES AND BITS

The most common, and probably most useful, bridle is a snaffle bridle which can also take a pelham bit, if required. Double bridles, requiring two headstalls to take the two bits – the bridoon (a thinner version of an ordinary snaffle) and the curb or Weymouth – are for experienced riders, needing skill to avoid inflicting pain on the horse.

Although snaffle bits are usually the simplest bits, giving a direct feel on the horse's mouth, they are not necessarily mild. This depends on how many joints (if any) there are in the mouthpiece and, as ever, how sympathetically the bit is used. Rough hands can cause a horse great pain even with the mildest bit.

The most common snaffle is one with a single joint in the middle of the mouthpiece, the mouthpiece being joined to a ring at each end, either by means of the ring passing through the end of the mouthpiece (loose ring) or by means of a covered joint inside a slightly bulbous shaping (eggbutt). An eggbut snaffle has the advantage of not being able to pinch the horse's lips but does give a more fixed feel in the mouth, which some horses like less than the looser feel of a loose-ring bit. See which your horse goes best in. Do buy a stainless-steel bit, not so-called 'solid nickel', which is very weak, bending easily and often cracking and breaking without warning. The type of metal will be

stamped on a good stirrup or bit somewhere where it won't rub or scratch the horse's mouth.

Another ostensibly mild bit is the half-moon or mullen-mouthed snaffle, either loose ring or eggbutt type. These can be made of metal but are more commonly made of rubber called vulcanite and all are good if of a reputable make. The shaping leaves less room for the tongue than an actual joint and the bit gives a fairly 'fixed' feel in the mouth but some horses do like these bits.

It is important to have *reins* that are comfortable in your hands as, otherwise, they will adversely affect your handling of them and, consequently, the feel you give the horse via the bit. Probably the most common reins are rubber-covered leather, which doesn't slide through your fingers when wet with sweat or rain. Try different widths to see which is most comfortable.

CLOTHING

You may not need clothing if you never clip your horse and provide it with excellent shelter facilities in stable and field. However, most people and horses value well-designed, good quality and correctly fitting clothing and you will find life easier if you have at least one good stable rug and one good waterproof turn-out rug. Ideally, you should have two of each to allow for laundering and drying but, particularly if your horse is kept on the combined system and you use synthetic rugs that will wash and dry overnight, you could manage with one of each.

Headcollars and ropes

A good-quality leather headcollar with a browband, which adjusts not only on the near-side cheekpiece but also at the throatlatch and noseband, is an investment you will never regret. The browband stops the headpiece sliding down the neck and creating a pull on the horse's nose, and the extra adjustment points allow for a perfect fit, something that is impossible with most other headcollars.

Leather will last more than a lifetime if well cared for but good synthetics are now available.

I dislike nylon webbing: it is rough on the skin, looks cheap and nasty and frays easily, when it becomes dangerous. Webbing is also extremely strong. This can be a drawback if you turn your horse out in its headcollar and it gets caught up somehow, as the webbing is virtually impossible to snap.

Try to find a strong *jute leadrope* rather than a softer, weaker cotton one, as the former is normally usefully long (at least 2m or 6 ft) and hard-wearing. You can buy one with a dog-lead spring clip or a trigger type; both are fine.

Two different ways of attaching a leadrope to a headcollar. On the left is a trigger clip and on the right a spring clip. They fasten *away* from the head as this is safer.

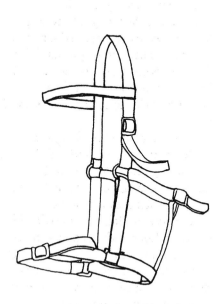

A good headcollar will have a browband and adjustment buckles on the cheekpiece and on the throatlatch and noseband.

A well-shaped modern stable rug with cross-over surcingles passing under the belly. These should be fastened, for safety and comfort, so that you can just fit the width of your hand between the surcingle and the rug.

Modern rugs of any kind should be 'horse-shaped', i.e. the back seam follows the undulating line of the horse's back rather than being cut in a straight line, which creates potentially injurious pressure on withers, shoulders, hips and croup. Also, they fasten by means of criss-crossing surcingles which pass fairly loosely under the horse's belly. This fastening, combined with good shaping and fit, means that the rug stays in place and is comfortable for the horse.

Old-fashioned rugs, which were often cut more or less straight down the spine seam, and were kept on by means of a separate roller or surcingle or maybe by a stitched-on surcingle, usually slipped round and back, often slid off down one side, and were very uncomfortable for the horse, particularly when it lay down and its trunk expanded against the unforgiving, fairly tight fastening. Withers were often rubbed sore and rugs trailed dangerously around the feet, sometimes tripping horses and bringing them down. Sadly, some horses are still rugged up in this awful way.

These days most *stable rugs* are made of quilted, synthetic fabric, and are often permeable to allow body moisture to evaporate through them, which means they can also be put on a wet horse, which will then dry off safely without ending up in a damp and clammy rug and will not need to be thatched with straw to assist in drying off. Cotton mesh 'anti-sweat' rugs, put on underneath usefully hasten the process.

Turn-out rugs, or *New Zealand rugs* as they are often called, are waterproof and intended for use by

The uncomfortable, old-fashioned way to rug up a horse, with a separate roller round its ribcage. If you do use this method you will find that the blanket stays on better if the folded point (behind the withers) is caught under the roller.

horses turned out in rain or muddy conditions. They are particularly useful for owners whose horses spend the day in the field while they are at school or work and although they are no substitute for a good shelter, they do make such horses' lives more comfortable.

They are available in synthetic fabrics but most are still made of traditional canvas. The same rules as to shaping and design apply as with stable rugs. Never buy the type of rug kept on by a surcingle around the horse's middle: they are most uncomfortable and easily slide out of position as the horse moves about the field or rolls. Once out of place, the

firmly fastened surcingle holds it there and the leg straps, which pass between the hind legs, are pulled up most uncomfortably into the groin on one side and hang down dangerously low on the other side. None of this happens with a well-designed, horse-shaped rug with leg-straps, crossing surcingles or an under-harness of some kind.

CARE AND STORAGE

Synthetic tack and clothing are undoubtedly much easier to care for than traditional materials. Synthetic saddles often simply need a brush and a sponge or hose down. Synthetic

A traditional canvas New Zealand rug. It is, as it should be, a roomy fit – passing over the root of the tail and extra deep to minimize draughts on the belly. It has a neck hood for added protection, which fastens to the neckline of the rug.

rugs can normally be washed on the medium cycle in a washing machine at 40°C (104°F) (if it will fit inside), although it is vital to follow the manufacturer's instructions to avoid possible damage to the fabric. Synthetic boots etc. can be similarly treated.

Leather should be washed with just-warm water (using a sponge), damp-dried with a chamois leather or something similar and then saddle soap (the glycerine type is best) should be rubbed firmly and thoroughly into both sides of the leather with a different, soaping sponge. You should damp the soap, not the sponge, as if you make it too

frothy nothing works properly. Pay special attention to parts touched by metal, such as under buckles and where the ends of the reins and cheekpieces pass round the bit rings. Ideally, you should clean your tack each time it is used to prevent hardened and weakened leather and sore horses.

If you use glycerine saddle soap, there should be no need to use special nourishing leather dressing unless your leather gets a real soaking or is being put away in storage.

If washing items that combine traditional materials such as wool (as in rugs or boots) or synthetics with leather, the warm water and mild soap will not damage the leather if you give it a thorough dressing with neatsfoot oil or a good brand of leather conditioner before and after washing. It is also important to rinse items in clear water really thoroughly and I like to add ordinary domestic fabric softener to the last rinse (again it won't affect leather) as it does help to keep all fabrics in good condition, unless the manufacturer's instructions advise against this.

When storing tack or clothing, it is best to take it to pieces and store it flat in drawers, chests or on shelves. Mothballs can be used if you wish but the resulting, lingering smell is offensive to most horses. Saddles should be stored on their racks, covered up against dust in a 'breathable' cover (in other words not nylon or plastic) as they keep their shape best this way. Any material, traditional or synthetic, is best stored in a dryish place at room temperature. Cold and damp ruin everything.

EQUIPPING A TACK ROOM

You should keep your tack and clothing in a dry place at about room temperature (roughly 20°C or 68°F). Apart from this, it's worth being security minded and, if possible, keeping it either in the house or in a tack room attached to the house, or taking other precautions against theft.

There is no need for a special building provided safety and temperature are considered. You should store your saddle on a proper rack. Your bridle can simply be draped over the saddle seat or hung on a semi-circular bracket, perhaps fixed to the wall beneath the saddle bracket. A thin peg or, even worse, a hook or nail in the wall, will soon spoil the shape of the headpiece and may even cause the leather to crease, crack and eventually break.

Rugs can be kept on brackets, clothes racks, shelves, in chests or anywhere convenient provided they

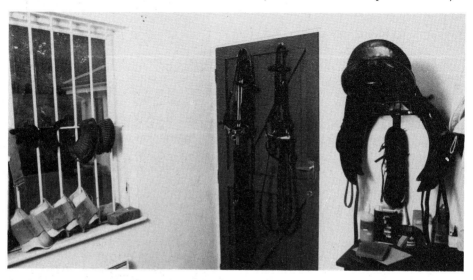

A well-kept tack room. Note the security bars on the window.

Left: A corner hay rack with mesh rather than vertical bars. Corner racks are safer as the horse is less likely to injure itself on them, and the mesh makes it necessary for the horse to pull out small amounts of hay which is less wasteful and increases the horse's eating time.

Below: A popular type of corner manger. It is easy to remove and clean, with a rounded bottom edge to prevent knee injury should the horse stamp while eating, and side bars to stop the horse scooping out and wasting feed.

Right: A water bucket and holder.

Below: An automatic waterer saves a lot of work.

Feed should be stored in galvanized, vermin-proof bins like these.

Keep your feed room neat and clean to deter vermin. Here, plastic bins are used for storing feed – a good, economical alternative to metal bins.

Flaked maize. Note its coarse texture and yellow colour.

Oats are best crushed, like this, for easier chewing and digestion.

Seed hay (*left*) and meadow hay (*right*). Seed hay is much coarser than meadow hay and is usually fed to hard-working horses. Meadow hay is used for more moderate work and for resting horses and ponies.

Hayage looks like hay but is moist and has a distinctive smell. To get your horse used to it, mix it in with hay. Mix in small amounts at first, gradually increasing the hayage over several weeks.

Cubes or nuts are usually of a green or beige colour.

Bran is expensive and of poor nutritional quality.

Bruised barley, shown here, is often better than oats for ponies, cobs, resting animals, horses of excitable temperament and those allergic to oats.

You can identify the various ingredients in coarse mix and, because of the added molasses or syrup, it is moist and darker than straight cereals such as oats or barley.

Sugar beet is an excellent feed for horses. It is grey in colour, dark grey if molasses has been added. *From the left:* cubes, shredded pulp or flakes, pulp.

A forage feed.

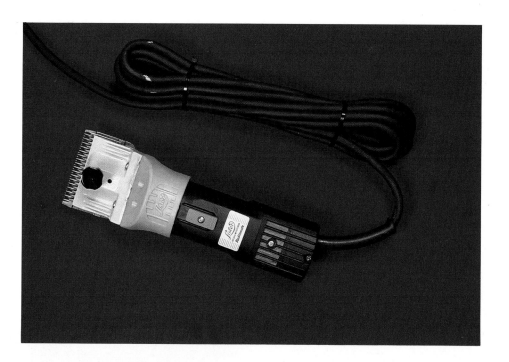

Above: A clipping machine. The blades must be kept clean, sharp and oiled. The horse must be clean and dry before clipping otherwise the process can be uncomfortable as the blades may become blunt and pull the horse's hair.

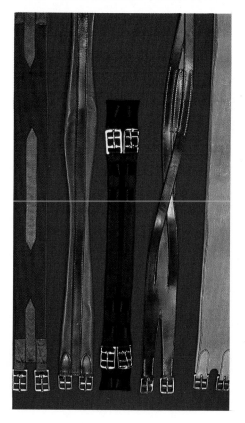

Left: Girths. *From the left:* Modern synthetic girth, Atherstone, belly/dressage girth, Balding, three-fold leather girth.

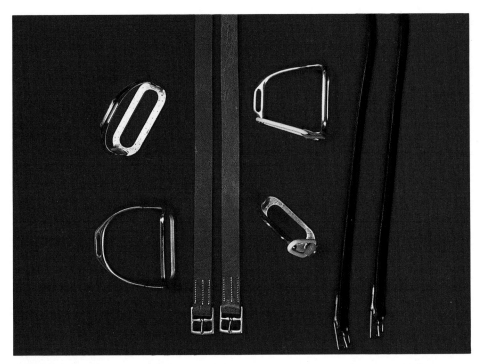

Stirrups and leathers. *From the left:* English hunting irons, buffalo-hide leathers, Peacock Safety irons and ordinary leathers.

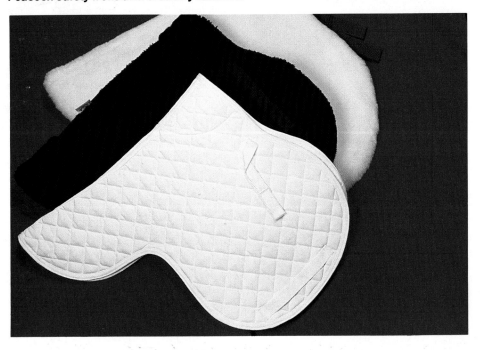

Two synthetic numnahs and a quilted cotton numnah (*front*).

A double bridle put up neatly on a well-shaped bracket to help preserve the shape and condition of the headpiece.

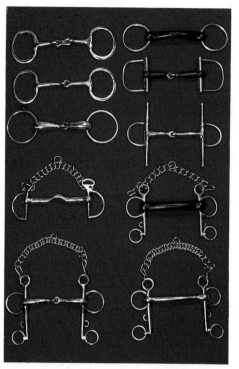

Left: A selection of bits. *From the top left:* Doctor Bristol snaffle, jointed eggbutt snaffle, wire-ring German jointed snaffle, ported Kimblewick, jointed pelham. *From the top right:* loose-ring rubber half-moon snaffle, rubber-covered D-ring jointed snaffle, jointed cheek snaffle, vulcanite half-moon/mullen-mouthed pelham, metal half-moon/mullen-mouthed pelham.

Below: A bitless bridle attachment with independently moveable cheeks for more precise aids.

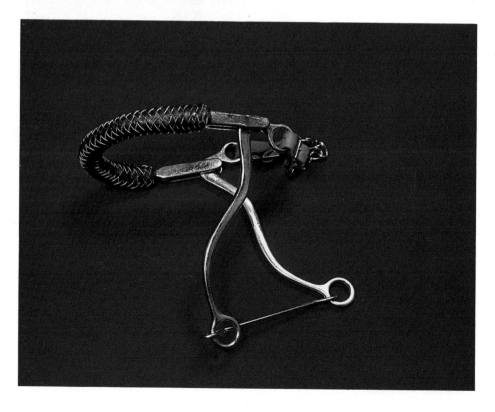

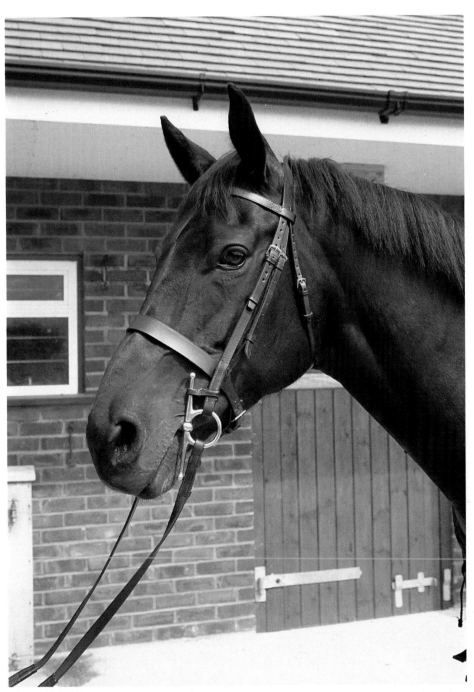

A comfortable, well-fitting bridle. The horse has plenty of room for its ears yet the browband is not too long and floppy. The throatlatch is loose enough to admit the width of a hand between it and the head, and the ordinary cavesson noseband is not rubbing up against the sharp facial bones and will easily allow two fingers beneath it.

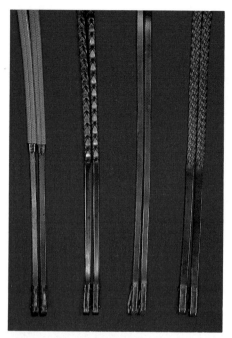

Reins. *From the left:* rubber-covered, laced, plain and plaited.

A general purpose saddle correctly put up on a plastic-covered bracket. The irons are run up the leathers and the girth is laid over the seat.

Overreach boots. *Middle:* The older type, which can be difficult to put on and take off and often turns upside down, becoming useless and dangerous. *Left:* This overreach boot has a fastening, making it easier to use. *Right:* The new petal type which is easy to use and cannot invert itself during use.

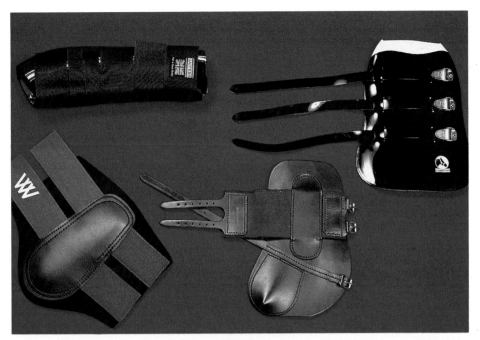

Boots. *Clockwise from the top left:* Synthetic brushing boot with Velcro fastening, synthetic boot with strap and clip fastenings, heel boot (which actually protects the underside to the fetlock) with an elastic insert for comfort and strap and buckle fastenings, fetlock boot with Velcro fastening.

Neglected grassland with tufty grass and lots of inedible weeds.

This Thoroughbred stallion looks alert and healthy, with a sleek, glossy coat.

A small, handy horsebox with haynets up, ready for the journey. This useful side ramp arrangement means that the horses do not have to back down the ramp, something most horses dislike or find frightening.

This two-horse trailer has a front exit ramp so that horses do not have to back down the entrance ramp at the rear.

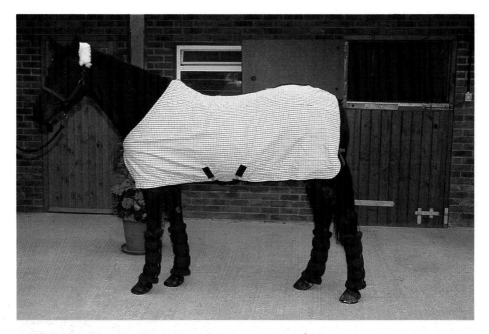

Dressed for travelling. The headcollar is padded but this is not as effective as a proper headguard which covers the whole of the vulnerable poll area. The rug is well designed and comfortable and the horse is wearing travelling boots. The horse will also need knee pads and hock boots.

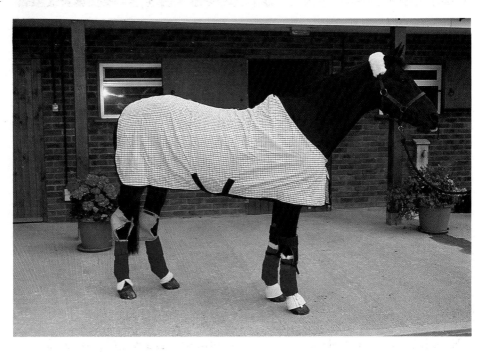

Properly dressed for travelling, wearing bandages and knee and hock boots.

Tack cleaning equipment. *Clockwise from the back left:* bucket, leather dressing/ conditioner substitute chamois leather, spray bottle of saddle soap, washing sponge, bar of glycerine saddle soap. You will also need a soaping sponge.

are kept brushed and folded. It is useful to have drawers or boxes to store boots, bandages and so on.

It is best not to use the feed room for storing tack as feed rooms are invariably dusty, which will affect your tack. In old stable buildings there is often a compartment or separate room for tack but stables are usually humid places and this, too, is bad for leather.

Common sense and a dry, fairly warm atmosphere are needed to keep tack in good condition and able to last a lifetime.

Running water is useful for cleaning, although many owners

clean their tack at home in the kitchen, not to mention using the domestic washing maching for clothing, boots and bandages. The latter should be washed inside an old pillowcase to prevent them from tangling up. Boots and rugs should have their fastenings done up to prevent them getting caught up during washing.

An old-fashioned clothes rack, which can be hoisted up to the ceiling of the tack room or kitchen, is a boon for drying everything, especially wet turn-out rugs overnight – although an airing cupboard is a good substitute!

CHAPTER 8

ACCOMMODATING HORSES

For a start, horses are creatures of the wide open spaces, although they do need shelter (see p.16). Their mentality dictates that they prefer to be outdoors because evolution has conditioned them to feel safer that way. In most of the western world, it has become accepted to keep horses mainly stabled, so many newcomers to the horse world think that this is best for horses. In fact, the reverse is true and in countries where horses and ponies are kept out much more there are far fewer management and psychological problems to cope with.

It is true that if they are kept in very small spaces, horses might injure each other when lying down or rolling, but in practice, it is simply untrue that horses that are friends will fight and bicker when kept in close contact.

The generally accepted parameter for yarding arrangements, field shelters and so on is that you should allow the space of one conventional stable for one horse and half as much again for each additional horse for very small numbers such as two to four animals. A more generous allowance should be made for larger numbers of horses.

Even if you do allow this space in an undercover, fenced-in yard, you will find that keeping horses yarded involves much less mucking out (droppings and very wet flooring/bedding material only being removed) and that the horses are much more settled, content and amenable to handling and work.

One research establishment I know of, run by a vet who is also a horseman, has indoor yards bedded with barley straw on earth floors. Urine drains straight through and once a week a tractor and trailer are brought in to remove the droppings and bedding. The atmosphere remains sweet and fresh, the bedding dry and the horses healthy.

If you do have to keep your horse or pony in a conventional stable, you can do much to ensure its health and contentment by altering the box so that the horse can see out on as many sides as possible, by fitting adequate ventilation devices as described on p.8 and allowing the horse to see, touch and chat to neighbours. Of course, only friendly horses should be stabled next to each other.

As for size, it is generally felt that a box of 3.6 × 3.6 m (12 × 12 ft) is about right for a 16 hh horse, although I regard this as *minimal*. The points to remember are that a horse needs at least half its length again

A line of conventional loose boxes made of brick, which is an excellent choice. Although the loose boxes have no ridge roof ventilation, there is plenty of room for rising stale air. The windows should normally be kept open as the doors do not provide sufficient air circulation.

Light

Recent research by Dr Houpt of Cornell University in the USA, has shown that horses are happy under a roof provided they have access to light when they want it and an all-round view, plus congenial company. Compare this to the normal situation – horses kept in single loose boxes that are the equivalent to prison cells, with no real contact with neighbours and no facility to switch on the light when they wish. Although horses have better eyesight in the dark than humans, this American study using horses taught to turn on a light when they wanted to, showed that they nearly always preferred to be in dim light at night than total darkness.

Their preference for a clear, all-round view of their environment is not surprising when we remember that they are prey animals and need to know what is going on all around them in order to feel safe and secure. Their preference for natural social contact with friends, colleagues and neighbours is already well known, although many owners disregard it.

(from nose to tail) to feel safe about lying down, turning round and rolling, that adequate ventilation is a health *must* rather than a desirable bonus and that horses in the wild always choose the driest place to lie and rest, so keep a strict eye on the bedding.

A rearing horse can easily reach a height of about 3.2 m (10½ ft) at the poll and, although it may not make a habit of doing this indoors, a horse needs plenty of headroom in order to feel secure. A height of 2.3 m (7½ ft) to the eaves, as is normally given in modern pre-fabricated boxes, is totally inadequate. A box with a single-plane roof (which should slope from front down to back rather than vice versa to give good drainage unless you have effective guttering along the front) should really be 3.2 m (10½ ft) at the lowest point at the back to ensure a good air space as well as a feeling of security.

You do not need to make your stable warm as horses do not mind cold, *dry*, *still* surroundings and you can always rug them up. There is no need, therefore, to have your box lined to the eaves, although kicking boards are a good precaution around the lower half and the roof should certainly be well insulated, more to protect against heat and condensation than cold. A verandah overhang protects human attendants and horses appreciate it in rainy weather.

All electrical fittings in boxes must be out of reach of the horses and of the waterproof/condensation-proof type for safety, with cables sheathed inside conduits, partly to protect against corrosive humidity and partly against inquisitive teeth.

American barn-type stabling, consisting of loose boxes inside a large building, usually with a central aisle, can create a more herd-like environment if the boxes are separated by grilles or bars, rather than solid partitions, but ventilation is often very poor in such buildings as the airflow is only down the centre aisle, while stale air collects in the boxes down the sides. Disease spreads more easily in such a design, so ventilation outlets must be used to the full and be set above the height of the horses' heads to avoid draughts directly on to the horses.

Stalls where horses are tied up all the time are half the size of loose boxes but this old-fashioned method of housing horses is not suitable for any horses on limited exercise, as most privately owned horses are. Indeed, most caring owners would not subject their much-loved animals to the restriction and lack of space enforced by this method.

THE OUTDOOR LIFE

Not only should paddocks be kept free of poisonous herbage, such as ragwort, but it is also good economy to allow grass to form a good part of your horse's diet. Good grass-seed mixes are available for athletic, working horses, so there is no need for grass to make horses soft and fat.

Many firms selling grass mixes and fertilizers will advise you free of charge on your maintenance and you can also contact independent consultants or (in Britain) the Equine Services Department of the Agricultural Development Advisory Service for advice on a good basic

American barn stabling with a wide central aisle to take a muck or feed trolley. Although the doors at each end can be kept open, ventilation can be a problem in these stables unless each box has its own inlets and outlets. Stale air tends to pool in the boxes as they are out of reach of the breeze wafting down the centre.

management plan that is suitable for horses, not cattle.

You should divide your land in two or, if possible, three or more paddocks, which your horses graze in turn, so that each part can be used, treated and rested, which is essential to keep it in good heart. Horses are picky grazers and will not eat anything they find distasteful unless, for instance, they develop a taste for something poisonous which they have tried because they are desperately hungry. In addition, they designate areas in their fields where they do their droppings. The grass here grows long and is wasted as horses do not normally eat near their droppings and urine patches. The areas they do graze, called lawns, will become overcropped and practically bare in a neglected paddock.

Good land management partly depends on removing droppings regularly (ideally daily), which also helps in parasite control. The eggs of internal parasites are passed out in droppings, hatch out and the horses then swallow the larvae to begin the cycle over again as the larvae move around inside the horse, causing internal damage, before settling in the intestine to suck blood and lay eggs. Picking up droppings and removing them from the field helps to break this cycle, along with properly administered worming medicines (anthelmintics) bought from your vet.

When the grass in your field begins to look patchy, move your horses on to another paddock and cut down the left-over grass in the 'lavatory' areas of the first paddock. Then apply whatever fertilizers and treatments (such as harrowing) that your advisor has recommended and leave the paddock to rest for a few weeks.

When the second paddock starts looking patchy, with long and short areas, move the horses on again, so that your land gets a good chance to recover and remain productive.

Fencing

Fencing is important, both for safety, so that your horses do not injure themselves on it, and for security, to keep them where they belong.

The best fencing is high, thick, prickly *hedging*, which also provides a good windbreak if it is on the windward side of a field. Grow your own hedging where the land is your own and in the meantime make do with manmade fencing.

Wooden posts and rails are probably still the best, if rather expensive. *Plain wire, kept taut* on wooden posts, can be good, while *dropper fencing* can also be safely used for horses. With any wire fencing, however, keep a pair of wire clippers handy, as it is possible for a horse to get a strand of wire caught between a shoe and foot;

the horse will struggle like mad to get free and may not only tear its foot badly but bring down the fencing as well. Of course, the chances of you being present with your wire clippers at just the right time are very remote, so try to avoid wire fencing if you can, unless it is the small diamond-mesh type inside wooden frames, which has been used successfully for years in the USA.

Flexible rail fencing (usually PVC) fastens to wooden posts and can be excellent. It can be used to patch up existing fencing or gappy hedges or to fence round a field temporarily as you can take it down and re-erect it elsewhere time and time again – ideal for owners who have to rent temporary grazing.

Electric wire fencing is used by many owners. It can be effective if horses are taught to respect it. Damp their noses, lead them up to the wire and encourage them to touch it. They will receive a crack of electricity unpleasant enough to warn them

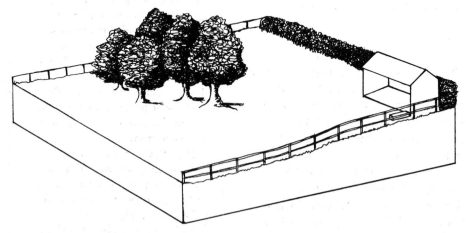

A good field will have a thick, high hedge on its windward side, overhead shelter from the trees and, ideally, a roomy shed with its back to the prevailing wind on the driest part of the field. It is better, however, not to site the shed in a corner as it is here, as horses milling around the shed may become trapped or injured.

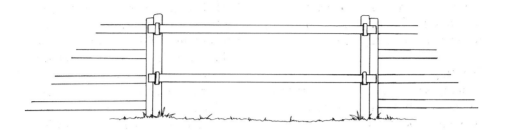

Sliprails are a cheap and effective alternative to a gate. There must be some means of securing them – usually a padlocked bolt or chain fastened tightly around the holders.

away in future but not to hurt them much. Fix coloured plastic bows or ties to the wire so that galloping horses, which do not see well, know where the boundary is. This is a good plan for any form of wire fencing.

Fencing materials to *avoid* are barbed wire (common but potentially lethal), chestnut palings, chicken wire, sheep netting, metal railing park fencing and plastic-covered chain-link fencing, all of which are either too weak or dangerous.

Gates

Gates and *sliprails* are needed, obviously, so that you and your horses can get in and out of the field but this also means that horse thieves can do so too. Gates should be strong, preferably with their bottom halves filled in with strong metal mesh to prevent horses getting their legs through the gaps and injuring themselves and/or breaking the gate. Gates should be strongly padlocked at both ends and be on capped hinges so that they cannot be lifted by thieves.

Sliprails are cheaper but less safe. You must secure at least one end by means of a strong chain that passes through holes in the rail and post and can be padlocked, while the other end sits in a closed holder. This will prevent horses from lifting the rail with their necks and prove time-consuming for thieves to deal with.

Identification

I believe that all horses should be identity-coded to deter theft. This can be done by means of freeze-marking, normally on the back, leaving a white code number, by microchipping, which involves a vet or trained operative inserting a tiny microchip into the horse's neck, or by having a special code number burned on to the hooves every few months.

Most firms operating such systems (they advertise in horse magazines) keep a central register and work in conjunction with the police, horse sales and abbatoirs, also offering a sizeable reward for information leading to the return of stolen horses and/or the successful conviction of thieves.

CHAPTER 9

EXERCISE AND WORK

Studies have shown that the horse mostly moves about at walk, and at a gentle amble for much of that.

From this, we can see that the exercise routine normally given to animals being ridden or driven bears little resemblance to the horse's natural lifestyle. True, we do accept that most of an exercise period should take place in walk but this is not the gentle amble that a horse in the wild or a field will use: we normally insist on a 'proper', smart walk, with the horse swinging purposefully along, up to its bit or not, depending on what we are trying to achieve, but certainly not 'slopping' along, achieving, to our minds, nothing much.

Much of a schooling session or lesson takes place in trot as it is believed that we can more easily achieve results in that gait. Furthermore, we often repeatedly lengthen and shorten the stride in trot, taking the horse out of its natural 'gear'. This means two tiring situations for the horse, first, spending a good deal of time in trot, and second, in a type of trot the horse would not choose for itself.

Perhaps we do a little better with canter, at least when out hacking, when we let the horse swing along naturally, this being the natural 'migration' gait for horses. Cantering in a restricted space, such as a *manège* or indoor school, is difficult for the horse and normally necessitates a slower gear within the gait than the horse would choose.

If this sounds rather bleak it is not meant to, but perhaps we can learn from it and amend our horses' exercise periods accordingly.

First, we should keep to the old maxim that most of an exercise period should take place in walk. We should certainly 'walk the first mile out and last mile home' when riding out, but should also spend much longer at the start of a schooling session in loosening the horse up in walk as opposed to the five minutes or so most horses get. Also, don't make it walk too fast.

Second, during a lesson we should not use trot as much as most people do, give the horse more rest periods of walking on a long or loose rein or simply standing still, and perhaps make more effort to discover and learn the feel of the horse's natural gear in this unpopular (with the horse) gait.

Third, remember more often how difficult the horse finds canter in a restricted space and, when out hacking, let it swing along more in its natural canter gear, rather than spending a lot of time in trot.

Centuries ago, the old horse-masters discovered that the way of going in which the horse can best carry our weight is to train it to carry itself with a little more weight on its hindquarters and to go with its head and neck, in fact its whole 'topline', 'stretched' or extended in a flowing, rounded shape with, in the young horse, the head down as opposed to poking up and out, and with the back relaxed and swinging rather than hollowed and tensed.

As schooling progresses, the horse is taught to bring its weight further back on to its hindquarters and the head and neck up more and in an attitude that we call 'collected'. Ultimately, the horse will acquire the strength and ability to go in self-carriage in that outline and there is no doubt that a properly schooled and strengthened horse is easily able to work in that fashion without any undue strain. Even so, appreciable periods on a long or loose rein, relaxing and resting, remain a vital part of any schooling session.

The need, both mental and physical, for plenty of movement is obvious. Horses that are short of exercise, particularly if over-fed with concentrates for the amount of exercise received, are often restless in the stable, which easily leads to the development of stable vices.

Its body often does not function optimally and it will often have that sadly familiar yearning, frustrated look so common in stabled horses.

FITNESS

Horses and ponies become fit in response to gradually increasing small stresses on the body in the form of more and more work. The body's natural response to stress of any kind is to strengthen itself against it so that it can bear it better in future. Then, when one particular level of stress can be coped with, a little more is delivered in the form of more work and the body again responds by strengthening itself, and so on for several weeks or months, depending on the fitness programme.

From a state of more or less complete unfitness, say, with a horse that has spent several months out of work, possibly at grass, it normally takes about six weeks to make a horse half-fit. Three months of correct, gradually increasing work will get a horse fit for almost any job and an additional month or so will bring it to the state of fitness needed for racing, three-day eventing or similar really hard work.

All horses have natural limits, beyond which they cannot be taken in a fitness programme, so not all horses, for example, can be made fit for, a 120 km (75 mile) endurance ride or a three-day event. Rest assured, however, that gradually increasing work, together with appropriate feeding, will fitten almost any horse provided it is not suffering from injury or sickness.

Getting a horse fit is not difficult and neither is keeping it fit. A fit horse needs less work to keep it fit than it did to become fit. Some owners send their horses 'over the top' and make them stale by overdoing the work once the horse is fit. The thing to do then is give interesting, varied and gentler exercise, while still keeping tabs on the horse's temperature, pulse and respiration rates to ensure its recovery rates, in particular, remain adequate.

It is certainly true that fitness is

essential for the horse to work safely. Unfit horses are weak, prone to stumbling, tiring easily and falling, and to injuring themselves when asked to perform work that is too much for them.

Half an hour's walking per day is not too much for a completely unfit horse. You can increase the exercise by half an hour a day each week until about two hours a day of increasingly taxing work is being carried out. So long as your progress is gradual, you will not harm the horse.

EXERCISE VERSUS WORK

Exercise may be defined as physical activity that the horse finds easy and which does not make it sweat unduly or breathe hard. The horse will sweat noticeably more on a hot or humid day than on a fresh or cold day: the areas that sweat most and are noticed first are the neck and shoulders.

Work, as opposed to exercise, will make the horse breathe harder and probably sweat more. A light hack of, say, two hours, mainly walking with some trotting, cantering and maybe a pop or two over easy fences can be regarded as exercise, whereas two hours of a good deal of cantering or galloping, jumping and so on while hunting can certainly be regarded as work. It is also fair to say that anything the horse does not particularly enjoy, or finds physically stressful, comes into the category of work rather than exercise.

Sometimes there is a fine line between work or exercise but a sensitive, knowledgeable owner will soon learn the difference as it relates to his or her particular horse. Also, as

a horse becomes fitter, work that would have considerably stressed it early on in its programme, can later be regarded simply as easy, enjoyable exercise because the horse is now physically able to cope with it.

Remember the useful old maxim: slow work is always beneficial, fast work rarely is. This means that unless the horse has an injury or is sick, you are never going to harm it with slow work – walking and steady trotting within reason – whereas cantering, galloping and jumping, plus fast trotting, are all more likely to overstress and injure a horse. There are obviously times during work or a fitness programme when we do have to give fast exercise or hard work in order to stress the body enough to respond to it, get used to it and enable the horse to go safely at that rate in future.

Unfortunately, it is often felt that because a horse has had its ridden exercise for a particular day, it does not need to be turned out as well. Your aim should be to ride or drive the horse according to its normal programme and also to turn it free *as well*, so that its day in domesticated conditions resembles as nearly as possible the type of regime it responds best to in nature and it receives both the physical and mental stimulation and satisfaction of movement and company. Long hacks in company best mimic the horse's natural exercise system and every effort should be made to arrange these for the benefit of the horses and the enjoyment of their riders.

CHAPTER 10

PSYCHOLOGY AND HANDLING

The horse's evolution has produced a very specific animal with a unique digestive system and a basically nervous mentality. This may sound strange when you remember the many 'bombproof' children's ponies, quietly entertaining and teaching their young riders or unflappable police horses keeping their cool under the most terrifying conditions, but it is true. The horse is essentially a pessimist, always on the lookout for trouble that may threaten its survival and usually acting first and (maybe) thinking later.

A herd life is ideal for a prey animal because there is safety in numbers. Packs of predators test a herd by harassing it to find out which are the weakest and slowest members, those most likely to be caught easily, so using up as little of the predator's energy as possible. Usually it is the young, old, sick or injured animals, and also pregnant mares, that are taken.

Predators often work at night, so the horse has to maintain a lookout 24 hours a day. This is obviously impossible for one individual, so they take it in turns to be on watch and always live in company whenever possible. In any group of horses, you will notice that some are grazing,

some dozing or lying down resting or sleeping and others casually keeping a lookout for danger. This happens in domesticity too. Walk down any row of loose boxes and you will find some horses resting, some eating and some on a kind of lookout. When one horse gets up, another, who may not even be able to see it, will lie down for its turn to rest.

The need for vigilance has created the horse's essentially nervous temperament. This also explains why the horse's lightning reflexes so often come into play without warning, such as when it shies. We can be grooming it quietly in its box when something suddenly startles it and it stands cowering at the back of the box or starts running round it in a flat panic, trying to get away from some danger, real or imagined.

It is essential for everyone working around horses to be confident and quiet (horses take their cue from us once they trust us). Always warn the horse when you are about to do something. Speak as you approach it, whether in box or field. Run your hand over its body, starting at the wither, until you reach the part you want to handle rather than suddenly, say, putting your hand on a fetlock and expecting the horse to lift its

75

foot. Speak if you are going behind it and touch it as you go, so that it knows where you are.

It is very useful to get the horse used to certain words and tones of voice, to which it will soon learn to react. Use, for example, 'No' in a firm, but not harsh, tone to correct it, and 'Whoa' or 'Easy' to calm it. Say 'Good boy' or 'Good girl' when it has been good but never to calm it as it will then think you are praising it for playing up. It is also a good idea to make the horse respond to his name. This is the first thing circus horses are taught and it is invaluable in bringing a horse's easily distracted attention back to you and the job in hand and away from fear or interesting diversions. Use the name when you want the horse to come to you, when you want it to listen to you and so on; keep at it until it really knows its name and *always* praise it when it responds.

I believe that rewards should be given as just that and never as a bribe. I don't like to give a horse a titbit when I first see it as I like to know that it is pleased to see me and not the titbit! Remember that 'Good boy' and a firm stroke on the neck are equally welcome rewards and perhaps only give food rewards at the end of a ride or schooling session or before a relaxed break during a lesson. Then the horse will understand and be willing to work again.

Because the horse's attention span is short, it is far better not to drill it for long spells but to work for short spells of only a few minutes, then let it have a reward and a rest for several minutes. This way you will keep it fresh and willing during work and avoid making it stale and sour because it will know the work never lasts very long.

SLEEP

Horses do not sleep for several hours at a stretch as we do but for about 30 or 45 minutes at a time round the clock, then waking and checking on the environment, eating and socializing when possible, before having another sleep, totalling about four hours out of 24.

This means that stabled or yarded animals should have enough hay to eat throughout the night as it is mentally upsetting and physically damaging for them to go for many hours without food passing through their digestive system. Yet, if you check in most stables late at night, you will almost always find that all the hay is gone and the horses are not due to be fed again for about eight hours!

Horses can sleep standing up. They have a 'locking device' in their elbows, knees and stifles, which props them up and enables them to rest one hind leg at a time, while the other three legs keep them upright and able to get away in an instant should danger threaten.

However, the type of sleep they can get standing, or lying propped up on their breastbones, is not as deep and refreshing as the really deep kind that they can only experience when lying flat out. This is obviously a very precarious situation for a prey animal to be in as it takes a horse several seconds to get to its feet and those seconds could be crucial in a life or death situation. This is why some horses always remain on watch to sound the alarm. It is why you should never barge up to a sleeping horse in a field or sneak up to its box. To alarm a horse that is lying flat out is just asking for trouble: it can quite easily go into a flat panic, trying to gallop away in fear, perhaps severely injuring itself or demolishing its stable!

Horses that are new to a yard may take several weeks before they feel secure enought to lie down in their new stable, let alone lie flat out to sleep properly and this can be because they simply feel strange or because the box is not big enough, the bedding not what they are used to and so on, so make allowances for this if the horse is not sleeping properly.

DISCIPLINE

Horses need kind, gentle handling: they are sensitive animals which respond brilliantly to this sort of treatment. However, discipline is also a necessary and natural part of their handling. They do not get all their own way in a natural or domestic herd environment. Foals are often severely disciplined, not only by other herd members but also by their own dams. Although horses are gregarious animals, they do not suckle each other's young, protect the young as a group or look after sick or old herd members. Each mare and foal unit regards itself as a separate entity and straying foals are kicked about by other mares. In fact, stallions are kinder to foals (provided they are their own – if not they may kill them) than are other mares.

Introductions

Correctly introducing a new horse to a herd is vital for its future relationships and contentment. Never bundle it into an existing herd and let it get on with it. This would never happen in nature and will result in the horse being kicked, battered and ostracized by the others. In the stable, put it next to two very friendly, meek neighbours and then turn it out with one of them alone at first, gradually introducing the other herd members one at a time over a period of days or weeks, the lowest in the herd hierarchy first, so that the new horse has a chance to make friends and find its own niche. Introduce the most dominant horses last and watch carefully to see who are going to be the new horse's friends and enemies so that you can manage them all accordingly in future.

Out hacking, ride the horse next to one of its friends and never put an enemy behind or closely in front of it.

Older youngsters, too, will keep foals down the hierarchy and foals are left to sort out their own positions in the herd. Dams will protect their own foals to a large extent.

This means that humans must keep the upper hand when handling an animal as big, strong and unpredictable as a horse. It is largely a case of mind over matter because no human can ever win a straightforward battle of strength with even a small pony.

Newborn foals should be left to bond with their dams for 24 hours before any real attempt at handling

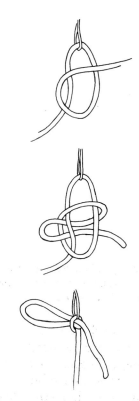

Tying a slipknot of half bow. It is not safe to thread the loose end of the finished knot through the resulting loop – if the horse pulls on it the knot will tighten and it could slow you down if you have to undo the knot in an emergency.

them takes place but once they realize who mum is and that they, the foals, are horses and not humans, gentle, correct handling should start while the foal is still weak enough to lose any arguments. The subject of handling foals is outside the scope of this book but is well covered in many good books on breeding and youngstock management.

Basically, you must let the horse know the word 'No', said firmly and strictly (but not shouted or screeched unless the horse is a really nasty piece of work, when a loud voice can certainly help bring it to hand),

means a form of punishment. Hitting the horse about the head is not a good idea. It can certainly make horses headshy and often does not work as a form of correction, even for biting. A sharp slap under the belly with the flat of your hand is much more effective as a general disciplinary action when 'no' is simply not proving sufficient.

If you come across a horse that is simply too much for you, it is well worth paying for professional help to sort it out. *Never* let anyone beat your horse up as this does not help and usually makes matters worse.

When issuing any sort of punishment, remember that it must be administered within *a second or two at the most* if the horse is to connect the punishment with the crime. If you leave it any longer, you may as well forget it – and if you do that the horse will think it can get away with it and do it again! Discipline must be administered instantly and faithfully *every time* a horse does wrong if it is to learn what is acceptable and what is not in dealing with humans. You cannot expect it to learn if you are inconsistent in your teaching.

Never vent your anger on a disobedient horse. Punishment, if administered, should be given in cold blood. People who cannot control themselves should not expect to control horses.

STABLE VICES

It is true to say that all stable vices are caused by humans. They stem from bad management or management that is inappropriate for the

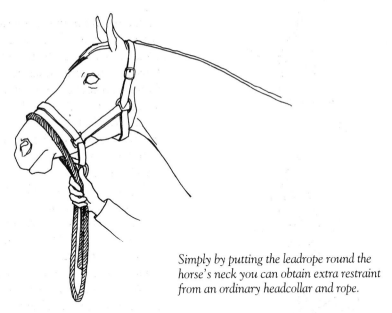

Simply by putting the leadrope round the horse's neck you can obtain extra restraint from an ordinary headcollar and rope.

individual concerned. Not all horses under a particular management regime will develop stable vices because some can tolerate that regime and some cannot.

Once established, most stable vices cannot be cured. Prevention is always better than cure and nearly all of the vices mentioned stem from incorrect feeding and over-confinement.

Crib-biting and *wind-sucking* are often the result of chronic

indigestion, probably due to insufficient roughage or straight-forward hunger. The horse sucks in air in an effort to get something inside it. Many people say that these habits *cause* indigestion and colic but it is more likely to be the other way round. Fewer concentrates and more hay (or its equivalent) are the answer and may stop the vice from becoming worse in the early stages or even stop it.

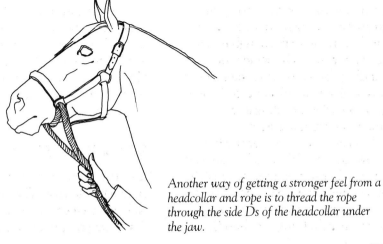

Another way of getting a stronger feel from a headcollar and rope is to thread the rope through the side Ds of the headcollar under the jaw.

Weaving and *box walking* are probably due to over-confinement and the lack of natural movement and exercise. They are also evident in unhappy, lonely, insecure horses (and zoo animals) deprived of not only movement and space but also close equine company. Many horses, when provided with congenial company and a more open environment (being yarded rather than stabled, for example, or properly turned out), will stop box walking and weaving during the reduced time they spend stabled, but many will always perform these vices in a stable even if they are only in it for half an hour.

There are tricky devices aimed at physically preventing horses from carrying out their vice – cribbing straps with a metal point that digs into the horse's throat when it tries to arch its neck to crib bite or wind suck, bricks suspended in the doorway of a stable to hit a weaver on the head as it swings its forehand from side to side, bales of straw littered around the track of a box walker and so on, but this approach is not the answer. As pointed out by Dominic Prince, a guest writer in my book *Behaviour Problems in Horses*, stopping a horse from physically performing its stable vice is tantamount to stopping a child from biting its fingernails by pulling out the nails.

If you have a horse with a stable vice, your best plan is to accept it as one of its imperfections and to manage it as naturally as possible, going to great lengths to do so if necessary. Ignore anyone who says stable vices are 'catching'. Many

years of experience tell me they are not. For example, if a whole yard of horses starts crib-biting, it is because the management in that yard is appalling, not because they are copying each other.

Interestingly, a survey among professional and 'serious' amateur horsepeople showed that they would not turn down a horse just because of a stable vice and few felt it really lessened its value.

Rug tearing is probably due to discomfort but it is surprising how many people do not seem to see this and make every effort to keep the horse from biting its rug (sloshing bitter-tasting liquids on it or even fitting the horse with a bib) but none of these things will improve the fit, design and feel of the rug, not to mention the condition of the horse's skin and coat.

My own view of rug-tearers is simply not to rug them up! In many cases, a horse can be clipped less, trimmed well and kept fit and in work without rugs. If it is adequately fed and housed (not in a stuffy, warm stable, either) with a good bed and sensible work, you may well find that rugs are simply not needed. When turning out, make sure the horse has a good shed that it is not afraid to use (watch for other, dominant horses keeping it out and remove them from its company) and I'm sure you will both be happy with the result.

It helps to accept that no horse is perfect and it is part of horsemanship to learn to cope with individuals' feelings and foibles. So often you can get round them with a bit of intelligent thought, consideration for the horse and common sense.

CHAPTER 11

HEALTH TOPICS

Well-managed and correctly cared-for horses have fewer health problems than those that are less fortunate. A contented horse, like a contented person or any other creature, thrives, fights disease, makes a quicker and more effective comeback after illness or injury, copes with work and stress and generally gets through life better than a neglected or mismanaged one. However, there are times when even the best cared-for horse or pony succumbs to disease or injury and responsible owners and managers take as much interest in sick horses as in healthy ones. It is essential to know what a healthy horse looks and feels like and how it behaves, so that you know at once when something is amiss.

THE SIGNS OF A HEALTHY HORSE

Ʊ The horse should look bright, alert and interested in its surroundings. If it is mainly stabled, it may spend time moping at the back of its box from boredom, but when you approach it should come over and express an interest in you. It should not seem nervous or full of nervous energy nor anxious or discontented. It takes some experience to spot the expression of emotions in a horse but

practice and sensitivity will help. Remember that a perfectly healthy horse can appear unhappy if it is badly managed, so make allowances for this.

Ʊ Its coat should be sleek and glossy and the skin beneath it elastic and moved easily over the ribs with the flat of the hand. The hair should generally lie flat, although it may appear ruffled if badly fitting clothing is rubbing it or it has dried in a ruffled position. Even grass-kept horses with winter coats should basically have sleek, quite bright coats that lie fairly flat and the hair should feel alive rather than stiff and lifeless. Hair that stands up away stiffly from the skin is said to be 'staring' and is a sign of poor condition.

Ʊ The eyes should appear bright with no abnormal discharge, although it is normal for a slight, jelly-like, greyish discharge sometimes to appear at the inner corners of the eyes. The eyes should not look sunken in their sockets and there should be no deep hollows above them unless the horse is old. This could also indicate that the horse is in poor condition.

U Ideally, your horse should be neither fat nor thin. The tables on p. 31 will help you to judge condition. For general, active work the horse should be well covered but lean enough to be fit and able to work safely. You should, as a guide, be able to feel the ribs quite easily but not see them: if you can see any more than the last two pairs near the hips the horse could be too thin unless it is a type that is naturally lean when very fit. A horse whose ribs cannot be easily felt is too fat even if it looks normal to you. A very obese horse or pony should be obvious to anyone and obesity is as bad for equines as for humans.

U The horse's action should be straight and true so that the hind legs follow directly in the path of the front ones, best checked by standing directly in front or behind. The natural action may be crooked however, so allow for this. Seen from the side, the hind hooves should land in the prints left by the forefeet in walk. In trot they should land in front of them, known as tracking up and over-tracking, respectively. If they don't it could be that the horse simply has poor action but if they normally do and suddenly do not, the horse could have a problem, such as lameness or back trouble.

Obviously, the hoofbeats should sound even: – one–two–

The correct way to trot up a horse is on a loose leadrope – to avoid restricting its action – and to hold the loose end in your free hand to prevent you or the horse treading on it and causing an accident. Trotting a horse up on a tight rope can disguise the natural action.

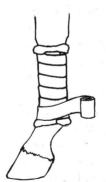

Exercise bandages. Place the padding evenly round the leg and start the bandages as shown. The flap hanging down is best covered with the first two turns of the bandage. Bandage evenly and firmly, but not tightly, down to the fetlock and back up, finishing just under the knee. Tie the tapes no tighter than the bandage itself to avoid pressure injuries and, if you use a bow or knot, tuck the ends in a fold of the bandage. Bandages tied in this way do not support the leg but may help to prevent some jarring and possible concussion injury.

one–two in trot, and with a slight hiatus between the beats in walk: one–two– –one–two– –one–two– –one–two. This is the normal rhythm: the regular one–two– three–four demanded by most instructors in walk is not the horse's natural rhythm.

If the horse is lame, this will be shown by uneven beats and you may actually be able to see lameness. The horse will dip its head lower when its sound leg comes to the ground and keep it higher when the lame leg hits the ground in an effort to keep weight off it. For the same reason, when an unsound hind leg moves, the point of the hock will appear to remain higher than the point of hock in the sound leg. It can be very difficult to diagnose lameness and this is really the vet's job.

When the horse is standing it should be able to stand square with all four feet evenly planted. It may often rest a hind leg with that hip down, but not a foreleg. Shifting feet around and looking uncomfortable is a giveaway of pain and lameness.

SIGNS OF AN UNHEALTHY HORSE

U The eyes and nostrils should have no abnormal discharges. It is normal for a slight watery discharge to appear at the nostrils but a watery discharge can also be an early sign of influenza, although in this case other signs would also be present, such as high temperature and lethargy. Thick, yellow or green discharges certainly mean trouble.

U The urine should be yellow and either clear or cloudy. Discoloured urine or urine that

83

smells unpleasant is certainly a bad sign. Droppings vary according to the horse's management system: those of a grass-kept horse will be greener and looser than those of a stabled horse, which will be khaki in colour and moist but not sloppy or slimy, and should just break on hitting the ground. Dark, pale, hard or very sloppy droppings or those containing slime or blood are certainly a sign of disorder.

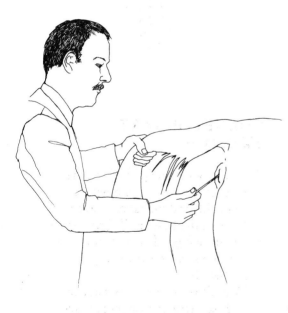

To take a horse's temperature, stand behind and slightly to its left (if you are right-handed), moisten the bulb of the thermometer with saliva or petroleum jelly and, holding the dock towards you with your left hand, gently insert the bulb into the rectum with a twirling movement from left to right. Push in the thermometer and leave it in place for the recommended time. Withdraw it, wipe it on the tail and read off the temperature.

ʊ The horse's appetite and thirst can tell you when it is out of sorts as it may go off its food or seem unable to chew or swallow it and may drink very little or too much compared with its normal rations. A horse can drink 54.5 litres (12 gal) or more on a hot day, particularly if working, so make sure this is available to it or you may actually cause illness through dehydration.

ʊ The horse's temperature will be about 38°C (100.5°F) at rest and will rise in work or sickness. A lowered temperature is also a sign of sickness. Old and fit horses have naturally lower temperatures than young or unfit ones. A variation of the at-rest level by about 0.5°C (33°F) warrants a call to the vet for preliminary advice at least.

The pulse rate in an average riding horse, weighing about half a ton, will be about 32–40 beats per minute, higher in smaller horses and ponies and lower in big horses. As with the temperature, it will be lower in fit and old horses and vice versa.

Respiration should be 'clean' and easy, any rough, rasping sound or a whistling or roaring noise on inspiration indicating trouble. The at-rest rate is about 12–20 breaths (in and out counting as one breath) per minute depending on the individual. Large and fit animals breathe more slowly than small or unfit ones. Pulse recovery rates were mentioned in Chapter 9. If at any time and for any reason the ratio of pulse to respiration reaches 1:1 call the vet at once as you

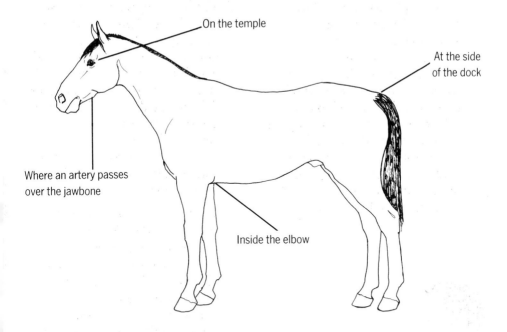

On the temple

At the side of the dock

Where an artery passes over the jawbone

Inside the elbow

Points at which to take the horse's pulse.

have a serious problem on your hands, whether from exhaustion or sickness.

Horses that have a problem breathing out, seeming to need a double, muscular effort to do so, could be 'broken winded' or suffering from chronic obstructive pulmonary disease (an allergic condition caused by dust and moulds). They often have a diagonal line running up the flank towards the stifle, caused by increased muscular development from the effort of breathing.

Temperature, pulse and respiration rates should be taken daily for a week before exercise, with the horse perfectly calm and at rest, at the same time each day, so that you get a reliable picture of your horse's norms. Any significant deviation in future can then alert you to trouble.

THE VETERINARY SURGEON

The vet is a very helpful ally in the task of maintaining your horse in good health and should not be seen only when the horse is ill. Preventive medicine and good management are the most effective way to keep your horse healthy.

Consult your veterinary surgeon regarding a vaccination programme against tetanus, equine influenza, possibly rhinopneumonitis and any other diseases which may be worth vaccinating against.

Your veterinary surgeon is also the correct person to advise you on parasite control in your horse. Internal parasites, commonly called worms, can kill horses and it is an essential part of good management to

To check respiration, stand just behind and to one side of the horse and count the rises and falls of the opposite flank. So, if you stand to the left you can easily see the movements of the right flank. Each rise and fall counts as one breath.

Worming

Most anthelmintics (anti-worm medicines) are now given in paste form in a plastic syringe and are squirted on to the back of your horse's tongue, although some are still given as granules in the feed. Vaccines against parasites are still in the developmental stage. The programme devised for your horse will depend on several factors – how many other horses are on the same pasture and how badly they are infested and with what, whether the parasites present have developed an immunity to any drug, which parasites are present, the time of year (worms are most prevalent in warm, moist conditions), the standard of your pasture management and so on. The most effective programme involves all horses and ponies being wormed at the same time every time. It takes only one infested animal to reinfect all the others, so you may have to use your persuasive powers to get other owners to carry out a proper programme for the sake of all your horses.

If you have trouble in this respect, your vet may well advise you to worm mainly with a drug called ivermectin which kills even larvae (young forms of parasites) still migrating through the blood vessels, unlike most anthelmintics which kill only mature worms in the gut. This will mean that your horse's level of larval parasite infestation is kept down and gets no chance to build up. Other drugs may be recommended occasionally to kill parasites not killed by ivermectin.

worm your horse with drugs at regular intervals as recommended by your vet.

The vet will also recommend six-monthly checks of your horse's teeth, which can wear sharp over time and make eating difficult, and he or she will then rasp (file) them smooth as needed. Youngsters need their teeth checking a little more often to ensure that milk teeth are being properly shed and permanent ones are coming through properly. Any horse can sustain a broken or diseased tooth, so dental checks are very important.

If your horse competes, and even if it does not, your vet may advise various blood tests and profiles, which will not only reveal a disease not yet discernible in symptoms (a sub-clinical disease) but the state of your horse's fitness.

Your first aid cabinet should be kept stocked with the best products available, purchased through your vet or a good veterinary chemist.

Finally, I feel it is essential for all owners to have at least one good, up-to-date veterinary book and to study it, then keep it handy for ready reference and 'refresher courses' when needed. I recommend *Understanding Your Horse's Health* by Janet L. Eley published in Britain by Ward Lock. Study such a book and the signs of good and bad health given in this chapter. Any deviation from normal should arouse your suspicions and you should ring the vet for advice at least. He or she will decide whether a visit is needed.

Ragwort is very poisonous and builds up in the body. It should be removed by hand and burnt. It is also poisonous to humans, so wear gloves and keep children away when destroying it.

CHAPTER 12

TRAVELLING

Travelling probably causes more trouble, fear and distress than anything else.

For a start, the horse is in an enclosed space which may be even smaller than its stable and possibly unable to see outside. The horse gets no warning when the vehicle is about to turn a corner, go round a roundabout, veer from lane to lane, lurch to a stop, speed up or go over a pothole or a bump. These things can be very frightening and stressful.

In addition, the horse may be very closely stalled next to one it does not know or even like. It is usually tied up and feels totally helpless, which is certainly geared to make it inclined to fight the situation as it certainly cannot flee. Many vehicles are also very badly ventilated, being either dangerously stuffy or uncomfortably draughty.

Ultimately, there is the very motion of the vehicle. Horseboxes are more stable, and generally safer than trailers, which sway and swing more and may be prone to jack-knifing.

The horse is built so that it carries about two-thirds of its weight on its forefeet, the hindquarters being the propulsive 'engine' and not meant to carry much weight.

Travelling horses has been the subject of a great deal of research worldwide and most of those involved in the trials now feel that the most comfortable and least stressful way to transport horses is with their tails to the engine, looking back in the direction from which they have come.

If facing forwards, when the vehicle accelerates, the horse's weight is pushed back on to its hindquarters, which have to brace to take the unaccustomed weight, and the horse also splays its legs unnaturally to help it to stay on its feet which is painful if maintained for more than a few seconds. Once the vehicle is going along at a constant speed (an unusual occurrence on the whole) the motion is even and the horse can stand naturally. When swerves, lane changes, turns and so on take place, the horse is lurched to one side, often with the vehicle slowing down at the same time. This again calls for braced muscles and splayed legs and also pushes the horse's weight on to its forehand to a greater extent than it is used to and which, to the horse, appears to put its delicate and fragile head at risk of being banged on the front of the vehicle. (Horses will normally do almost anything to protect their heads and feet.)

Roundabouts are particularly bad as the vehicle turns to enter them, curves round them, turns to come off them and then straightens up again, all combined with braking and accelerating and possibly bumps in the road, too. Bumpy rutted tracks on arrival at venues are also common.

When a horse is travelled facing the rear, acceleration is not so much of a problem as the weight is pushed on to the forehand and acceleration is usually not so violent as braking: when braking does occur, the horse's strong, fleshy rump is placed to take the impact, whether real or imagined by the horse. Turns can still be a problem but, in practice, it has been found that horses are better able to cope with them if facing backwards.

Although there is more to this topic than can be covered here it makes sense to travel your horse in a rear-facing stall in a horsebox whenever you can. With trailers, in Britain at least, this will be found to be very difficult as there are no rear-face trailers on the ordinary market: they have to be made to special order. You cannot just convert the inside of an ordinary trailer as the axle balance has to be carefully assessed and changed, otherwise the extra weight of the horse's forehand at the rear of the trailer can lift the front end up and the towing vehicle with it!

Whether the animals are travelling facing forwards or the rear, but especially the latter, the best advice is to drive as though you had no brakes. This will certainly slow you down and make all changes of speed and direction very gradual indeed, which will help the horses to adjust and avoid bad scares, which could put them off travelling in furture.

Another tip is to imagine that you have a glass of fine wine balanced on your bonnet, filled to within half an inch of the rim. If you spill any you will have given your horses a rough ride!

The constant use of muscles uses up energy and produces metabolic toxins or waste products, particularly lactic acid, in the same way as a severe physical workout. These toxins circulating around the system can cause painful muscle cramps and even muscle damage, producing a horse that, on arrival, is not only very stiff but also already tired and may even not be in a fit condition to compete. Very careful driving can alleviate this situation.

It is also vital to arrange your ventilation so that the horses are travelling in a cool, oxygen-rich atmosphere if the rapid development of dangerous bacteria is to be avoided. A muggy interior means too much carbon dioxide in the atmosphere, which gives the horse a headache and sleepy feeling; this, combined with the motion of the vehicle, can easily cause travel sickness. Unfortunately, however, unlike people, the horse is physically unable to vomit so it cannot relieve itself of this horrible feeling.

It is better to have the box a little too cool (although not draughty) than too stuffy as you can always warm the horse up with clothing.

CLOTHING

It is usual to bandage or boot the horse's legs for a journey and most people also bandage the tail and rug the horse up to protect it against rubs, either with a light sheet of cotton or linen or something warmer, depending on conditions. An antisweat rug

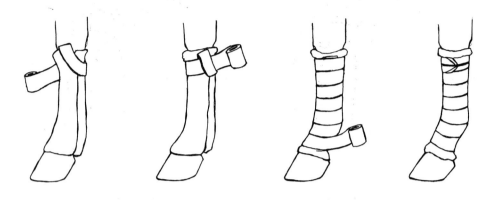

Stable or travelling bandages are put on like exercise bandages (see p. 83) but continue right over and under the fetlock, round the pastern, and back up again. They are mainly used for warmth and for drying off the legs and can help to control minor swelling. The bandages should be just tight enough to stay on comfortably.

under any rug helps to keep the horse dry. (If you feel under the rug and the horse is warm and damp, it is too hot; if you feel under and it is in a *cold* sweat, it is sick or frightened.) A poll guard completes the wardrobe for a journey.

The legs can be protected with stable bandages over padding, knee and hock boots and overreach boots (perhaps all round to minimize the effects of treads, which can happen to all four feet), or you can also use all-in-one travelling boots, which protect the entire leg from knee or hock right down over the coronet.

The tail bandage may have a tail guard fitted over it, which, in turn, fastens by tapes to a loop on the back edge of the rug or somewhere on the spine seam or, if you use the old-fashioned method of rugging up, to the rug's roller.

The type and weight of rug used should be determined by the weather and conditions inside the vehicle.

To accommodate the poll guard, the horse will need a good headcollar, preferably with a browband. The poll guard can be made of a rigid frame with padding and a leather cover, or can be synthetic, much lighter and ventilated. Some people wrap padding round the headstrap of the headcollar but that is a very poor substitute for a proper guard and does not protect the actual poll itself so it is really almost pointless.

For travelling, the horse must wear:

ʊ Travel boots or travel bandages over padding plus knee and hock boots;

ʊ Overreach boots;

ʊ A poll guard and headcollar;

ʊ A tail bandage and possibly a tail guard;

ʊ A sheet or rug, depending on the weather conditions.

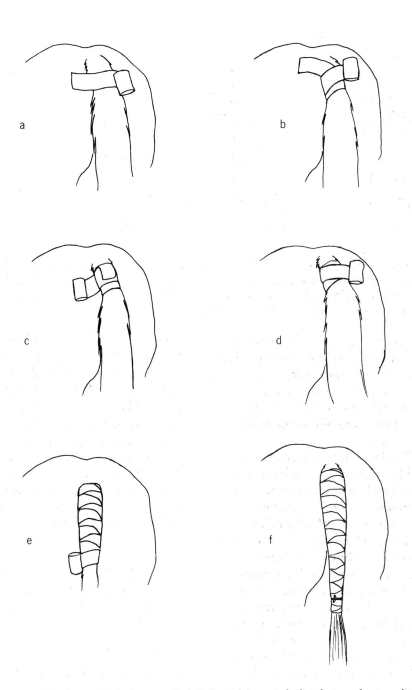

To put on a tail bandage, slightly dampen the hair first, then start the bandage as shown or by putting it under the dock. Leave a flap as for leg bandages and bandage firmly but not tightly over it before continuing down the tail. The start of the bandage should be right at the top of the dock. Finish about two-thirds down the dock, tying the tapes no tighter than the bandage itself, and finish by bending the tail into a comfortable shape for the horse.

FEEDING AND WATERING ON THE JOURNEY

Horses should be checked and watered every two hours on a journey. If possible, and provided a *safe*, convenient place can be found, unload them, let them walk about, stretch their legs, graze, stale and do droppings. Few horses will stale on a journey but many will do droppings.

A popular system is to give horses a haynet to munch at during the journey. On long journeys, short feeds should also be given at the horse's normal feed times. The longer your trip, the sooner before work you should aim to arrive, particularly bearing in mind the possible physical and mental effects of a journey. A good general plan is to arrive *at least* two hours before work is due, following a journey of about three hours, provided you have given the animals as smooth a ride as possible.

On arrival, offer another drink and quietly walk the animals around, perhaps wearing rainsheets if it is raining. It is important to get the circulation going gently to help to clear the effects of the journey, prepare the body for work, wear off any stiffness and so on. Don't leave horses in the box on a hot day but stand with them in the shade.

You can safely leave food and water with the horse until an hour before you start working in. Do have hay, feed and water (preferably taken from home in a large container so that its taste and smell are familiar) ready so that you can feed your horses correctly during the day, keeping to as normal times as the day's events allow.

Once home again, do not fall into the old trap of giving a bran mash for reasons already explained on page 32. If the horse is tired, half its normal feed will do, with the rest later, but give it as much hay as it wants. The horse should be given about six swallows of water every 15 minutes until it is cool, and then *ad lib*. An electrolyte drink should also be available to the horse.

TRAVEL TRAINING

One good way to do this is to get horses used to vehicles from foalhood, by having them about or even leaving them in the paddock so that they can investigate them at will. Often, a ramp is let down and the horse's feed put inside. Some people like to lead their horses around the vehicle then up the ramp, following another reliable horse, or the foal's dam where appropriate, into the vehicle and out the front entrance again, if there is one, or turning round in the box and coming out again.

Backing a youngster out can be very difficult but is necessary in many trailers. It is an advantage to teach the youngster to back on the ground first so that it will obey the command in the trailer. It is often necessary for a helper to put a hind hoof gently down on the ramp and to allow the horse to turn its head slightly so that it can see where it is going. Again, following another animal down helps, as does scattering bedding over the ramp to make a familiar surface. Teaching animals to back down a ramp is a job for the experienced as so much can go wrong. Where there is space, it is always better to let the youngster turn round and come out forwards, although there may come a day when, as it grows, it will have to learn to back out.

For the journey, have a familiar, friendly, experienced travelling companion. Initially, just start the engine, let it run for a little, then unload again. Then you can start on very short, very careful trips and gradually build up. It helps to have someone in the back of a horsebox plying the horses with titbits but remember that it is illegal in many countries for humans to ride in a moving trailer.

The way the horse's mind works means that just one unpleasant experience can put it off travelling, maybe forever, but a bad experience can be overcome if the first few experiences are good, so do everything possible to ensure this. Scientific tests have shown that if you can get a horse to associate a particular activity with something pleasant, such as its favourite food, it will take to it willingly.

OVERCOMING COMMON PROBLEMS

Initial training methods are also used to help to overcome fear in an animal that has had a bad experience and become difficult to travel. One thing is sure, even if you feel your horse is being stubborn rather than afraid, beating it up will only convince it even more that travelling is evil and to be avoided.

Instead, put it through the usual training programme and reward it copiously when it does well. Remember, however, that sometimes

a fright or bad experience is so deeply ingrained in an animal's mind that you cannot overcome it, so always check this when you buy a horse.

Refusing to load up is probably the most common problem encountered and if you simply *have* to load, say, to come home from a show, try two rather forceful but not painful methods. The best known is to fix two lunge lines to the sides of the trailer or lorry and have two assistants gradually cross them behind the horse's thighs, pulling them tighter and tighter to push it fairly unavoidably up the ramp where someone is waiting with its favourite titbit.

The second is to have an assistant ready with a stiff-bristled yard broom with which he or she scrubs the horse under the tail, firmly but not roughly, the *instant* it baulks. This, like the lunge-rein method, usually works.

Playing up during the journey can be difficult to deal with and you may have to stop to calm the horse down. Calming voices and a hand stroking the neck calms many horses but never go into the compartment as a panicking horse is extremely dangerous. Careful driving, a view out and a quiet companion are often the answer.

Refusing to unload is rarer but can, again, be dealt with with the yard broom in an emergency or, preferably, with lots of patience and titbits. When hesitating horses do decide to go (often after someone has put a hoof on the ramp), they may do so with a leap, so be ready to go with them. Have a friendly horse at the base of the ramp and a titbit waiting.

Backing out too soon can be stopped

simply by not undoing the breeching chain or bar until the horse is untied and you are ready to go down. Few horses will run backwards down a ramp. Calming voices and assistants at both sides of the ramp, guiding and steadying the horse, are a great help.

Whatever the situation, always remain calm, confident and *keep your temper* as creating a noise and getting frazzled will make things worse as this frightens horses and a frightened horse cannot think of anything but its fear and getting away.

THE CORRECT WAY TO LOAD AND UNLOAD

Lead your horse in a straight line straight up to the ramp, letting it follow you by walking at its head rather than its shoulder to give a lead, if this helps. Believe it will go in and it probably will. Try to have your vehicle parked downhill so that the slope of the ramp is lessened and make sure it is light inside, with plenty of bedding down and on the ramp. Haynets hung up and a friend loaded first always help. Have your gates up on each side of the ramp and try to park with one side of the ramp against a wall if you are expecting trouble and lead the horse from the other side with a schooling whip in your outside hand or a helper at its hip but not within kicking distance.

If the horse stops, lead it away again at once and turn it in a couple of little circles at the foot of the ramp, then straight up again. Inside, tie it just short enough that it cannot interfere with neighbours but not so long that it can get a foreleg over its rope.

To unload, put down the ramp and open the gates and make sure you have room in case the horse rushes down. Untie it, then have someone undo the breeching chain or bar and back down carefully or lead confidently forwards and down, depending on your vehicle. Walking at the horse's head often helps.

Looking back at a hesitant horse staring into its face or pulling on the leadrope are all guaranteed to stop it dead in its tracks, so look where you are going and don't think of problems, then you probably won't get any.

If you do experience serious problems with travelling, as ever it usually pays to hire a professional to advise you and maybe retrain the horse. By 'professional' I mean not only a professional money-wise but a sympathetic, knowledgeable and truly expert trainer. Never let anyone beat your horse up or be rough with it as this will certainly convince it that travelling is to be avoided at all costs. Calmness and confidence usually win the day in the end.

INDEX

Page numbers in *italic* refer to the illustrations

Action 82–83
Alfalfa 29
Apples 30
Arab horses 12, *12*
Auto-waterers 15–16

Balanced diet 24
Bandages 83, 89, 90, *90–91*
Barefoot horses 38–39
Barley 24, 27, 29
Barn-type stabling 68, *69*
Bedding 41–45, *41*
Bits 59
Blanket clip 51, *52*
Blood circulation 34–35
Body brushes 48, 50
Bodyweight 30–31
Boots 90
Boredom 14, 21
Botulism 26
Box walking 80
Bran 28–29, 92
'Breast 'n gullet clip' 53, *53*
Breathing 84–85, 86
Brick floors 42
Bridles 59, 64
Brushing 48, 50
Buckets 15–16

Cantering 72
Carbohydrates 27
Carrots 30
Cellulose 21–22
Chaff 26
'Chaser clip *52*, 53
Chop 26, *27*
Clean-air regime 42
Cleaning tack 62–64, *64*
Clipping 51–53, *51–53*
Clothing 59–62, *61*, 64, 89–90
Coarse mixes 28, 29
Coat 46–53, *47*, *51–53*, 81
Cold-blood 11, 12, *12*
Colic 14, 21, 79
Combined system 9
Company 18, *18*
'Complete' diets 24–25
Concentrates 13–14, 22, 25,
    26–30, 33
Concrete floors 41–42
Concussion 35
Condition 30, 82
Constipation 29

COPD (Chronic Obstructive
    Pulmonary Disease) 25, 85
Crib-biting 79, 80
Cubes 27–28, 29, 30
Curry combs 50

Dandy brushes 49–50
Deep-litter bedding 44
Dehydration 15, 84
Diet 13–14, 21–33
Digestive system 13–14, 21–22,
    21
Discipline 77–78
Drainage floorings 41–42
Dropper fencing 70
Droppings 22, 43–44, 45, 69, 84

Ears, trimming 55, *55*
Electric wire fencing 70–71
Electricity 68
Enemies 19, 77
Energy 23, 32
Evolution 10–12, 66, 75
Exercise 8, 14, 19–20, 72–74
Exercise areas *10*, 20
Eyes 81, 83

'False' feeds 29
Farriers 35–38, 39, *40*
Fats 23
Feeding 21–33, 92
Feet 34–40, *34*, *37–39*, 49
Fencing *18*, 70–71
Fetlocks, trimming 54, *55*
Fibre 23, 24–26
Fields 16–17, 68–71, *70*
Fitness 73–74
Flexible rail fencing 70
Flies 17
Floors, drainage 41–42
Fly repellents 17
Foals 77–78
Fodder beets 30
Food 13–14, 21–33
Forage feeds 14, 24, 29–30
Freedom of movement 19–20
Freeze-marking 71
Friendships 18, 19, 48, 66, 67,
    77
Full deep-litter 44

Gaits 19–20, 72, 82–83
Gates 71

Girths 57
Grass 9, 13, 22, 29, 68
    hydroponic 32
Grooming 46, 48–51, *48*, *49*

Hay 14, 21, 22, 24–26, 33, 53,
    76
Hayage 14, 24, 25–26
Haynets 25, *26*, 92
Headcollars 60, *60*, 79
Health 81–83
Hedges 16–17, 70, *70*
Herd behaviour 18, 75, 77
Hoof conditioners 40
Hooves 34, 36, *37–39*, 40
Horseboxes 88–94
Hot-blood 11, 12, *12*
Hunter clip 51, *52*
Hydroponic grass 32

Identity codes 71
Illness 83–87
Irish clip 51–53, *53*

Jaw, trimming 54, *56*
Jute leadropes 60

Knots 78

Lameness 83
Laminitis 35, 38, 39, *40*
Laxatives 28–29
Leadropes 60, *60*, 79, *82*
Leather, care of 63–64
Lighting 67
Lignin 22
Lipknots 78
Loose boxes 8, *8*, 19, 66–68, *67*

Maize 24, 27, 29
Manèges 20
Manes, grooming 50, 54, *54*
Micro-organisms, in gut 21, 22,
    29
Microchip identification 71
Minerals 23
Molassed chop 26, *27*
Molassine meal 26, 30
Movement, freedom of 19–20
Muck heaps 45
Mucking out 43–45, *43*

Names of horses 76

New Zealand rugs 61–62, 63
Nostrils 83
Numnahs 57–59
Nuts 27–28

Oats 24, 26–27, 29
Oils, in diet 23

Paddocks 16–17, 68–71, 70
Paper bedding 42, 43
Parasites 69, 85–87
Peat bedding 43
Personal space 17–19
Phytin 26–27
Poisonous plants 69, 87
Poll guards 90
Post and rail fencing 70
Praise 76
Proteins 23
Przewalski horse 12
Psychology 75–80
Pulling manes and tails 54, 54
Pulse rate 84–85, 85
Punishment 78

Quartering 50–51

Ragwort 87
Reins 59
Respiration 84–85, 86
Rewards 76
Rolling 46
Roots 30
Ropes 60, 60, 79, 82
Roughage 13, 21, 22, 23, 24–26, 33, 79
Rug tearing 80
Rugs 59–62, 61, 62, 63, 63, 64–65, 89–90

Saddle pads 57–59
Saddle soap 63, 64
Saddles 57, 58, 62, 64
Sawdust bedding 42, 43
Schooling 72–73
Semi deep-litter 44
Shampoo 48, 49
Shavings, bedding 42–43
Shelters 16–17, 70
Shoes 35–38, 36–38, 40
Silage 26
Skin 46–48, 81
Sleep 76–77
Sliprails 71, 71
Snaffle bits 59
Space 17–19
Sponges 50
Stable rugs 61
Stable vices 21, 25, 73, 78–80
Stables 7–9, 41–42, 66–68, 67, 69
Stalls 8, 68
Stirrup irons 57
Stirrup leathers 57
Stomach 13
'Straights' 24
Straw
  bedding 41, 42, 43–44
  feeding 24, 26, 33
Succulents 30, 33
Sugar beet pulp 26, 29, 30, 30
Surcingles 61, 61, 62
Sweating 74

Tack 57–65
Tack rooms 64–65, 65
Tails
  bandages 90, 91

grooming 50
pulling 54, 54
Teeth 87
Temperature 84, 84, 85
Theft 71
Thermometers 84
Trace clip 51–53, 52
Trace elements 23
Trailers 88–94
Travelling 88–94
Trees, shelter 16–17
Trimming 53–55, 54
Trotting 72, 82
Troughs, water 15, 16
Turn-out rugs 61–62

Urine 41, 42, 43, 45, 69, 83–84

Vaccination 85
Ventilation 66, 68, 89
Vets 85–87
Vitamins 23

Walking 72, 74
Washing rugs 63–64, 65
Water
  drinking 14–16, 32, 84, 92
  hosing down 48, 49
Weaving 80
Wind-sucking 79, 80
Wire fencing 70–71
Wooden posts and rails 70
Work 74
Worming 69, 85–87

Yarding 7, 10, 66

Zero-bedding systems 41